Praise for

"Parenting Is Your Highest Calling"

"Few things can cause a more steady stream of self-doubt, guilt, and fatigue than parenting. This book is a glorious light at the end of the tunnel! I wish Leslie had written this book twenty years ago. What she has written will free all of us to parent with joy, clarity, and freedom."

—NANCY ORTBERG, author of *Looking for God: An Unexpected Journey through Tattoos, Tofu, and Pronouns*

"Quite apart from her deeply thoughtful, candid content (as a mother of five I recognize reality, knowing a bit about parenting myself), Leslie Fields's writing about the myths of parenthood is literally superb, full of nuance, anecdote, passion, and skill. Her book gives counsel that is authentic and penetrating."

—LUCI SHAW, author of *What the Light Was Like* and *Breath for the Bones;* Writer in Residence, Regent College

"I could write a book about how much I love this book. Instead, I'll try to sum it up in a few words: *Yes! Thank you! Hallelujah! Amen.* Leslie Leyland Fields gives reason to cheer to all parents who've ever felt like losers, failures, or altogether bad Christians because of the destructive myths our culture and (gasp!) churches peddle about what good parenting entails. Flying right in the face of those lies, she offers a gracious, encouraging, and honest picture of what God longs for from us as parents—and as his children."

—CARYN DAHLSTRAND RIVADENEIRA, author of *Mama's Got a Fake I.D.: How to Discover the Real You Under All That Mom* and columnist for *Today's Christian Woman*

"Leslie Leyland Fields releases parents from the difficult, sometimes guilt-producing myths and mind games all of us play about raising a family. This book is practical, hope-filled, energizing, and very beneficial."

—JIM BURNS, PH.D., president of HomeWord and author of *Confident Parenting, Creating an Intimate Marriage,* and *The Purity Code*

"Finally—a book that leads parents out of guilt and inadequacy to worshiping God instead of the family and loving children instead of trying to be the perfect parent. My only regret is that this book didn't exist twenty years ago when I needed it."

—JAN JOHNSON, author of *Invitation to the Jesus Life* and *Living a Purpose-Full Life*

"After reading Leslie's book, I exhaled, hugely relieved to find out I wasn't alone in my private doubts about the 'be all and end all' of motherhood. I also rejoiced to learn the whole truth: that parenthood isn't just a series of warm fuzzy rewards but rather something deeper and much more complex. If you want to offload the false pressures and expectations of parenting, and find out what God *really* wants for your family, keep reading."

—LORILEE CRAKER, mother of three and author of ten books, including *Through the Storm: A Real Story of Fame and Family in a Tabloid World* with Lynne Spears

"*Parenting Is Your Highest Calling*' provides refreshing and needed encouragement to moms and dads. Chapter 8 is worth the price of the book alone. I heartily recommend it."

—KEN R. CANFIELD, PH.D., founder, National Center for Fathering

"Leslie Leyland Fields offers counsel to parents that is liberating and demanding and theologically profound: be faithful to God and trust in God alone. Especially in a culture that assumes we have the ability to fix everything, including the lives of our children, this is good news."

—BEN C. OLLENBURGER, professor of Biblical Theology, Associated Mennonite Biblical Seminary in Elkhart, Indiana

"Thank goodness for Leslie Leyland Fields, who dares to speak a word of truth against a lot of nonsense. Christian parents burdened by guilt and shame will find here blessed relief, based in the Bible and in hard-won experience of God's grace. Let this book equip you to say a firm 'no, thanks' to these nine parenting myths and all the others like them."

—DEBRA RIENSTRA, author of *So Much More: An Invitation to Christian Spirituality* and *Great with Child: Reflections on Faith, Fullness, and Becoming a Mother*

"Most parents are overcommitted, overtired, and overwhelmed. 'Amen and Amen' to this no-nonsense book on parenting! *This* Mrs. Fields skips the cookies and milk and the oft-recycled platitudes. Instead, she boldly and biblically serves the meat and potatoes that all moms and dads so desperately need as we attempt to nourish ourselves and our precious children. She deftly debunks nine myths and reveals nine truths that will change the way you view parenting."

—ELLIE LOFARO, speaker, Bible teacher, and author of numerous books, including *Spaghetti for the Soul*

"Parenting
Is Your Highest
Calling"

"Parenting Is Your Highest Calling"

And 8 Other Myths That Trap Us in Worry and Guilt

Leslie Leyland Fields

WATERBROOK
PRESS

"Parenting Is Your Highest Calling"
Published by WaterBrook Press
12265 Oracle Boulevard, Suite 200
Colorado Springs, Colorado 80921

ISBN 978-1-4000-7420-4

Copyright © 2008 by Leslie Leyland Fields

Library of Congress Cataloging-in-Publication Data

Fields, Leslie Leyland, 1957–
   "Parenting is your highest calling" : and eight other myths that trap us in worry and guilt / Leslie Leyland Fields.—1st ed.
       p. cm.
Includes bibliographical references.
   ISBN 978-1-4000-7420-4
   1. Parenting—Religious aspects—Christianity. 2. Parenting—Biblical teaching. I. Title.
   BV4526.3.F54 2008
   248.8'45—dc22

                                        2008029527

Printed in the United States of America
2008—First Edition

10 9 8 7 6 5 4 3 2 1

To Naphtali, Noah, Isaac, Elisha, Abraham, and Micah

You have, every one, enriched my life beyond measure.

Contents

Acknowledgments

As I sit down at the end of this project, I am profoundly grateful. Every piece of writing consumes personal resources, but some require more. This book has required much from my family, especially my husband, Duncan. I am so thankful for his understanding and support offered at so many levels. My children have sacrificed as well and have been remarkably patient with me throughout this three-year-long process. (I promise you homemade desserts again, and the chance for you to beat me at cribbage and rummy!)

My editor Elisa Stanford has been an uncommonly smart and stalwart companion through this entire process, from the initial idea to its final expression. I could not have done this without her. Laura Barker, too, has enriched this book through her wisdom and support. Questa Harper stepped in and lent her quick mind to this project. My agent, Greg Johnson, has been incredibly responsive to needs along the way. Every reader will benefit from their excellent work.

I am hugely indebted, as well, to the many friends and parents all over the country, and especially here in Kodiak, who have shared their family lives and struggles with me. You have inspired, motivated, and taught me. Some have given special encouragement by reading and responding to cover designs and earlier drafts: Debbie Bastian, Joy Ng, Renee Lyons, Suzanne Jensen, Ben and Stephanie, Ann Voskamp, Susan Underwood, my sisters Laurie and Jan, and many others. A special thanks for Beth Fields (for too much to name!). Thank you all for your investment of yourselves and your time!

Most of all, I am grateful to God and the power of his living Word. Attempting to speak truth from his Word is the most exciting and yet the most daunting, fearful task I know of. He has kept me through the most ordinary days of hard work and the most harrowing days of need. He truly has been my ever-present Savior and Sovereign. I am relying on his work even now, that as these pages are turned, his words will accomplish all that he purposes and desires.

Parenting Doesn't Have to Be This Hard

I am going to bed happy tonight. We've just had a family meeting on our bed—all five boys and our daughter sprawled, folded, draped limb to limb across the bedspread. We talked about our upcoming plans to travel for the year, about schoolwork, about the church service the day before. Naphtali, our oldest, will be off to college soon. The boys were cooperative, listening and contributing to the conversation. Our eldest son was showing increasing maturity. The two sons in the middle were getting along better than usual. Abraham and Micah were still the darlings of the family. I managed to ignore the turf war Isaac and Abraham were having at the foot of the bed. We ended with reading a few verses from Acts and with my husband, Duncan, praying the day to a close. Everyone trotted off to bed cheerfully.

I want cameras rolling, recording these moments against all my self-accusations and guilt. I want evidence proving what great parents we are. I feel affirmed, ready to broadcast my love for my children to the world, ready to write a book on how to parent well.

But if I am honest, I can't end here. I have to tell of other moments, like the morning this book began. Everyone was squabbling and ignoring my instructions. In the rush to get all six kids out the door to school, anger and morning sloth collided: accusations, eruptions, tempests filled the air. These were the themes of the week—and of my life at that point.

When everyone was safely away in their own calmer environments, I went for a walk in a dense spruce forest near our home. Failure weighed heavy on my shoulders—again. I had sent everyone off that morning, not with loving words of affirmation, but with words of anger, impatience, and sarcasm. My mind raced through the maze of questions I knew by heart: Why wasn't I a more joyful and loving mother? Why were my children so lacking? Why did I always feel like a failure? And how could I pray honestly about all this to God? How many children had he raised?

> Why wasn't I a more joyful and loving mother? Why were my children so lacking? Why did I always feel like a failure?

I knew the rational answers to some of these questions. Raising six children—a daughter and five sons—was my life's work, and yet it was work that often pushed me beyond my own limits. I could rattle off the challenges in a single breath:

I live in a harsh climate (Kodiak, Alaska) with five boys indoors much of the time through long, dark winters. My boys are not bookish, placid, or reserved. My husband travels often, so I am holding down the fort more than either of us ever wanted. And though we had planned for a family of four children, in my forties two more came—surprise children who enriched and complicated already overwhelmed schedules and lives.

Yet for all this, I knew my life circumstances were in some ways ideal. My husband and I are still married after more than thirty years. Duncan and I desire to please God with our lives. We are healthy. We love our schools, our church, our community. So why, after twenty years of parenting, is raising our children still so challenging?

How Could God Know?

I was not alone in asking these questions. Perhaps these family scenarios sound similar to yours:

- Your precious three-year-old wakes up one day and decides he wants to run his own life. He doesn't need you. The two of you, who once shared one body, are now wholly separate.
- You're a homeschooling mother. You've given your life completely to your children, stepping away from responsibilities at church and work so you

can fully serve your family. You wonder if you will have any other ministry again. Where is the personal fulfillment you expected from this work?

- You're a single parent, trying to support your two children. You have to put your younger child in day care. This was never part of your parenting plan. You ask yourself, *How can I raise my kids to be godly adults when I'm absent so much?*

- Your teenage son will barely speak to you. He is angry and distant. You struggle to love him—you hardly even like him right now. But admitting these feelings brings guilt. You thought you would always feel a deep love for him, as you did when he was an infant. What happened?

- You have a special-needs child who requires constant care. You love her, but this is not what you signed up for. You feel as though you've given up the life you and your wife desired. Resentment seeps in, then guilt.

- You're parenting the best that you know how, guided by best-selling Christian books, but your children are not responding. Why aren't they happy and content? What are you doing wrong? Why can't you create the peaceful Christian home so many promise?

If you believe the parental angst and fatigue you feel is yours alone, consider this: In a survey conducted by Focus on the Family, the most frequent comment from mothers was that they felt like failures.[1] Author Julie Ann Barnhill writes of leading a parenting group and being so struck by the levels of guilt and insecurity that she asked if there was anything the parents *didn't* feel guilty about. Total silence ensued.[2]

Yet in many parenting groups, especially in church settings, parents are reluctant to speak the truth about their feelings and experiences. In a culture that increasingly devalues children, Christians fight to preserve biblical values of devotion to God and family. We who have unerring truth to guide us surely cannot feel overwhelmed. If our children are gifts from God, then how can we resent their takeover of our lives? If we can do all things through Christ, then nothing is too much for us to handle. How can we doubt? How can we question what everyone tells us is the greatest calling of our lives?

> Ironically, pretending that parenting is easy diminishes the value of family.

Ironically, pretending that parenting is easy *diminishes* the value of family. As truth seekers and truth speakers, we need to be honest about the cost of parenting. None of us—no matter the depth of our faith, the extent of our research, or the number of nieces and nephews we have—truly knew all that would be required of us when our first child came through our doors. No words, in fact, could ever ready a man and woman for the lifelong work of parenting.

Yet not many of us have examined our own parenting assumptions and expectations, holding them up to the unsparing light of the Scriptures. In the absence of biblical truth, we quietly absorb the "truths" our culture offers us: Children are here for our happiness. We're born with a natural instinct to love sacrificially. And if we simply devote ourselves to our parenting, our children will turn out as we want.

These were some of the silent voices I wrestled with that day in the spruce forest. But then came an answer to my emotional challenge to God: *How do you know what it's like to be a parent?* It came as knowledge I had long possessed but never stepped into, like a pair of boots sitting by the door. I realized that God did indeed know how it felt to be a parent. I mean *know* not because of his omniscience, but *know,* as in lived, experienced, felt. Know from the inside out. God knows how I feel as a parent because he himself is a parent. He is my own heavenly Father, of course—and I a daughter who often, surely, disappoints him. This alone should be enough to tutor me in God's own disappointments in parenthood. But there is far more. Fully three-fourths of the Bible tells the story of God's fathering of the people of Israel, whom he tenderly called "my firstborn son" (Exodus 4:22). In the book of Malachi, God rebuked his unruly children, saying, "A son honors his father, and a servant his master. If I am a father, where is the honor due me?" (Malachi 1:6).

God identified himself as a mother as well, assuring his people, "As a mother comforts her child, so will I comfort you" (Isaiah 66:13). In Proverbs, Wisdom (as a personification of God's wisdom) is feminine. And in the New Testament, Jesus compared his emotions to those of a mother (see Matthew 23:37). Throughout the Bible, God identifies himself as our heavenly parent, filling the roles of both mother and father.

That day in the forest, I remembered that the Old Testament records God's parental relationship as one of great desire, incomprehensible love, unending compassion—yet Israel's response to this perfect parental love was disobedience. One particular verse leaped out at me: "All day long I have held out my hands to an obstinate people" (Isaiah 65:2). In these words I found an astonishing reversal that quelled my tears and continues to bring amazement, comfort, and freedom.

In this verse, and throughout the Scriptures, we seldom see God as a happy, blithe parent. We see instead God hungering for more. God, whose every purpose stands, who "is

not served by human hands" (Acts 17:25). The almighty
God, ruler of the universe, who holds kings' hearts in his
hands. This same God reveals himself to us as a hurting and
tender Father who longs for a deeper relationship with his
children. We see God, the All Sovereign, choosing to make
himself vulnerable to the whims and sins of his fallen children. We see God allowing his heart to be broken again and
again by our failures. What kind of God is this? Not a God
lessened in omnipotence. Not a God who has failed as a parent, though our twenty-first-century criteria might suggest
otherwise. This is a God who understands all of my longings,
frustrations, anger, and hurt for my children—and yours as
well. God himself has been there.

WE ARE IMPERFECT BUT WE ARE NOT FAILURES

When we turn our eyes away from our culture to the reality
of God's own parenthood, and to the biblical narratives of
other mothers and fathers, we find truths about parenting
that challenge our contemporary preoccupations. When we
look beyond the few select verses we often focus on, we see
that parenting is more than five easy steps or three prayer-filled
strategies. We realize that loss and heartache often accompany
laughter and joy, even with the easiest child, and that though
we are imperfect, we are not failures. Scripture exposes our

simplistic notions of love and suggests that some of our goals for a Christian home may be based on history and tradition, or even our own convenience, rather than on God's truth. Above all, Scripture returns us to our highest calling: to love the Lord our God first, before all others.

These recognitions brought me immense hope—and a hunger to discover more. As I searched God's Word in more depth and breadth, and as I listened more closely to myself and to other parents, I began to find words for the silent assumptions I had long held close but had never expressed. I had assumed that unconditional love was a single, unwavering emotion. I had assumed, like many in our culture, that my husband and I were the makers and shapers of our children—that if we did our part right and performed well as parents, we would be rewarded with happy, godly children. I believed that fulfillment and joy would characterize all parenting and that if we hit a few problems along our parenting path, we would always find solutions. After all, doesn't God's Word promise all of this?

I have discovered that God's Word promises something far different—far greater—than my feeble assumptions. God's truths about parenting are as glorious and freeing as God himself, while our own half-truths are as human and limited as we are—and they hoist a crushing weight upon our backs.

The freedom God offers us is not like the world's freedom, which often means escaping from family responsibilities. Instead, God's truths call us back to our families with renewed commitment, love, and hope—hope that blooms from a whole pattern of thought, word, and action revealed throughout the Scriptures.

> God's truths call us back to our families with renewed commitment, love, and hope—hope that blooms from a whole pattern of thought, word, and action revealed throughout the Scriptures.

This book is not a manual to change your child: it is a deep gaze into the parenting heart of God our Father. As I wrote it over the past three years, my parenting challenges have increased, not diminished. My children—at present a twenty-year-old, three teenagers, a first grader, and a preschooler—are each wholly themselves, each with normal struggles that challenge me daily. Yet I have emerged from this writing process with a clearer and deeper faith in God's purposes for me and my children—and for the first time in twenty years of parenting, with more hope and joy than guilt. My life as a parent is forever changed. May yours be as well.

For Reflection and Discussion

Read Exodus 4:22 and Isaiah 66:13.

1. Do you think of yourself as God's child? Why or why not?

2. What words or images come to mind when you consider God as a parent?

3. What do you feel most thankful for as a parent today?

4. What do you feel most guilty about as a parent today?

5. How might your parenting experience change if you believed that God has experienced some of the same parenting hopes, frustrations, and joys as you have?

Myth 1

Having Children Makes You Happy and Fulfilled

Discovering God's Real Purpose in Giving Us Children

I recently received a sardonic e-mail accusing me of "blissfully pumping out babies" while the world is overpopulated and starving. I asked for it, in a way. I had written a cover story for a major Christian magazine defending the large family. The e-mail was long—but when I came to the word "blissfully" I had to smile. Clearly the writer did not have children.

I thought the same B.C.—Before Children. In quiet hours I imagined blissful days with my little ones, cherubic angels whose pudgy hands would reach into the chocolate chip cookie dough with mine, who would sit enthralled with my every story. We would make snowmen in the driveway, then drink hot chocolate with marshmallows that would stick to our chocolaty mustaches. We would make our own valentines by hand and take long hikes in the woods and mountains. All of this, amazingly, has happened. And so much more! My e-mail correspondent was right—parenting has moments of bliss and beauty, when children deliver great happiness and fulfillment to their parents' lives.

But how many of us tell the whole truth—that these moments do not define our lives with our children? That weeks, months, and sometimes even years go by when happiness and fulfillment through parenting are hard to find? I have friends whose walk through parenthood has been far more challenging than mine—and others' have been far easier. Some friends look at me blankly when I speak of the hardships, frustrations, and betrayals of parenting. These are usually parents who are either still new to the job or whose children are now adults, with the hard years of toddlerhood and adolescence well behind them. I am glad for these friends. I need the optimism they share on both sides of child rearing. But I know that the majority of us in the trenches now would confess to a more complicated set of feelings.

EXPECTATIONS MEET REALITY

As I solicited stories for this book, a mother of a large family wrote to me after a particularly bad day at home.

Before children, I thought parenting would be an opportunity to do things the "right" way—a Christian home, loving discipline, a nurturing environment. After all, we had God on our side, so it would all end happily ever after. Then reality starts to rear its ugly head—sleep deprivation for decades at a time, rebellion, tempers, depression, and weariness that doesn't seem to end. No, this isn't what I bargained for, I will admit it. There are times when I wish I'd never signed up, when it's difficult to see God working, and I feel so hopeless.

I heard from Janice, an educator and retreat leader who thought she would love playing Candy Land on the floor with her two young children. But she doesn't. And now she's wondering, since she wanted children for so long, why don't the daily tasks of motherhood bring her the joy she expected?

Kyle and his wife adopted an older girl into their family and found their home profoundly changed, weighted with the grief of their new daughter's difficult past.

Jerri left a promising career to have children, and she loved the move from career to home-making. But by her third baby, she was stretched so thin that she began longing for her other life.

Carl and Sandra tell me of their eldest son's divorce—a possibility neither of them had anticipated.

I know all of these parents well, and they are wonderful mothers and fathers who love their children enormously. Every one of them could tell of many joys along the parenting road. Yet all confess to the unforeseen reality that children can bring as much hurt as happiness, as much frustration as fulfillment.

This question of fulfillment in parenthood has become a flash point among feminists, Christians, and parents of all stripes. Authors Susan Douglas and Meredith Michaels write in their book *The Mommy Myth*: "We are fed up with the myth—shamelessly hawked by the media—that motherhood is eternally fulfilling and rewarding, that it is *always* the best and most important thing you do...and that if you don't love each and every second of it there's something really wrong with you."[1]

But should any of us measure the value of parenting by our levels of happiness? Here's the question that matters: Does God's Word promise us happiness and fulfillment through our children? Only through a hard look at Scripture do we find the answer to this question—and the real purpose to our parenting.

DOES THE BIBLE PROMISE HAPPINESS THROUGH OUR CHILDREN?

If anyone had asked me that question fifteen years ago, I might have quibbled with the word "promise," but I would probably have answered yes. I would have cited the verse most quoted by parents, Psalm 127:3–5: "Sons are a heritage from the LORD, children a reward from him. Like arrows in the hands of a warrior are sons born in one's youth. Blessed is the man whose quiver is full of them." I might have quoted Psalm 113, in which the writer praises God for his care of his people: "He raises the poor from the dust and lifts the needy from the ash heap.... He settles the barren woman in her home as a happy mother of children" (verses 7, 9). And there I would have stopped.

These are wonderful verses, revealing the value that the psalmists placed on children. Yet I wonder if we have made too much of their implications. Early in my parenting, I expected children to *feel* like a reward—like a hot fudge sundae after running a race, like a prize after finishing a difficult test. Instead, raising children feels much more like a marathon, like the difficult test itself!

I assumed for years that these verses were representative of others. But as I have undertaken word searches and studies, it now appears to me that little more in God's Word promises happiness along with children. The Bible does not exhort us

> Early in my parenting, I expected children to *feel* like a reward—like a hot fudge sundae after running a race, like a prize after finishing a difficult test.

toward children for the sake of our own fulfillment. In fact, we are given several stories of women whose hopes for happiness through their children led them astray.

We see Sarah, Abraham's wife, so certain that she would be fulfilled through a son that she ordered her servant Hagar to sleep with Abraham. She was tired of waiting for God; she had to have a child!

The nation of Israel was created through two sisters, Leah and Rachel, competing for happiness through children. As Leah delivered one son after another, Rachel became so frantic for children as a means of validation and fulfillment that she cried out to Jacob, "Give me children, or I'll die!" (Genesis 30:1). Her words became prophetic; she did die while birthing the son whom she named (while dying) Ben-Oni, meaning "son of my trouble."

We are given the story of another couple as well, a couple who had every reason to hope for fulfillment through their child. The book of Judges tells the extraordinary story that has so much to teach us about parenting, about happiness, and ultimately about God's sovereign purposes.

High Expectations

The story begins here: "A certain man of Zorah, named Manoah, from the clan of the Danites, had a wife who was sterile and remained childless. The angel of the LORD appeared to her and said, 'You are sterile and childless, but you are going to conceive and have a son.'"

The angel's promise came with this admonition: "Now see to it that you drink no wine or other fermented drink and that you do not eat anything unclean, because you will conceive and give birth to a son. No razor may be used on his head, because the boy is to be a Nazirite, set apart to God from birth, and he will begin the deliverance of Israel from the hands of the Philistines."

The woman ran to her husband to tell all that the angel had said. Imagine their excitement! She repeated to him the special care she had to take. No fermented drink, nothing unclean, "because the boy will be a Nazirite of God from birth until the day of his death," she told him, breathless, still almost not believing.

The angel appeared a second time, this time to Manoah as well, and repeated his earlier instructions. Manoah and his wife were so grateful that this angel had come that they insisted on presenting a burnt offering to him. As the smoke from the fire went up, the angel of the Lord ascended in the flame. Husband and wife fell to their faces. "We are doomed to die! We have seen God!" (see Judges 13:2–5, 7, 22).

This is how their parenting journey began. What expectations they must have had. What joy and excitement they must have felt! It would have been enough to have any child to end their barrenness. Any child would have brought happiness, all that they longed for. But a child whose coming was announced by God!

Even without angels in our stories, most parents at one time have felt a wild leap of joy in their hearts to hear that a child was coming. Along with that child, we expect the arrival of joy, completion. Where did this hope come from? Probably not from the mouth of an angel but from a much less heavenly source: the culture we live in, both our mainstream culture and our church culture.

THE ALL-AMERICAN PURSUIT OF HAPPINESS

American culture is founded on the right of every citizen to "the pursuit of happiness," as our Declaration of Independence affirms. This, coupled with our culture's individualism and the wealth we have to fund our tastes, fuels almost continually within us a fixation with chasing our pleasures. We look to consumerism, status, fame, a six-figure income, and a six-pack body as just the starting list. *But will it last?* Christians ask. We condemn these pursuits as fleeting and unspiritual, and then we offer our own solution. "You want true happiness and fulfillment? Stop chasing after meaningless things that can never satisfy. Put your energies into something that provides real satisfaction and eternal rewards: your family."

For me and for many Christian women, the church has

been the most insistent voice urging us toward family as the means of fulfilling our needs. My daughter, a student at a Christian college, reports that many of the young women she knows are anxious to find a husband and begin a family because that is where they assume they will find completion. Countless parenting books emphasize that God intends motherhood to be more joyful and rewarding than any other experience. What have we done? We have traded one error for another.

We do it again from another angle. As we fight for the sanctity of life—through the issues of abortion, stem cell research, medical ethics, and euthanasia—we are battling what appears to be a declining value placed on children and life itself. The church has risen up to proclaim the inherent worth of life. I am one of those who stand up to shout these truths to any who will listen. But sometimes, as the words filter down to the pew, to the radio listener, and to the page, the message goes askew and children are offered as instruments for our own gratification. To persuade others of the value of children, we speak glowingly of the blessings they bring.

I heard this in nearly every interview I did for my previous book on unexpected pregnancy.[2] I would begin the interview by describing the emotional terrain of unplanned pregnancy. So many women experience despair, depression, and fear as they face a child they had not planned on. I experienced the same emotions through my last two pregnancies, both in my forties. Then the radio host would inevitably ask, "And now, aren't you so happy you have those children? Aren't they blessings from God?" Yes, every one of my children is a huge blessing to Duncan and me! I can't imagine my life without them. But these questions are mostly irrelevant. Even if my children had not brought me happiness, they would still bear the image of God, they would still be created by God, and they would still be of infinite value. It is not the state of my feelings that determines their value. Their value is found in the God who made them.

I fear that in our zeal to protect the family we end up affirming the value of children based on the wrong standards. Like the rest of our culture, we still consider happiness to be our highest goal; we simply replace the means to achieve it. Our goals move from our career to our home, from our own advancement to our children's advancement, from our salary to our progeny.

So, if children are not here for our happiness and fulfillment, what are they here for?

WHY DO WE HAVE CHILDREN AT ALL?

So much is against the enterprise of parenting. After all, God's command to Adam and Eve to be fruitful and multiply appears to have been more than fulfilled. And having children today defies personal economics. Web sites coolly calculate the cost of raising a child at anywhere between $150,000 and $1 million each.[3] Children simply cost too much—and not just in dollar figures. They undo us. They show us how much and how little we're made of. It often seems that they come only to break our hearts. And we let them. We invite it all. We admit perfect strangers through our doors and decide to love them wildly, without condition, for as long as we live.

How do we account for this behavior? For most of us, in our most selfless heart we have children because we want to learn to love as God does. For me, this longing hit at age twenty-eight, while I was tunneling into the heart of the Congo on the back of an expedition truck. Suddenly I was unutterably weary of my own small life and my own endless requirements for self-fulfillment. After eight years of adventuring with my husband—through world travel, graduate school, and life in the Alaskan wilderness—I understood instinctively and theologically that until I poured out my life to others, my own desires would enslave me. I wanted the paradoxical freedom that comes from sacrifice, from giving my life away. I remembered that unless the seed that falls to the ground dies first, no life-giving plant will ever grow. I believed loving others is an essential part of our created humanness. I wanted an intimate, lifelong, indissoluble relationship with others, the kind of life that simultaneously sucks you dry and sustains you. I believed children would deliver this—an extravagant, ambitious, love-filled, others-centered life. As they have.

At the heart of our desire for children, then even beyond our hopes for happiness, is the longing to love. I see the fruit of this in my own life almost every day. Today, for instance. Right now I am tired. Very tired. Duncan has been gone for two weeks while I've managed home and children. Tonight I have a choice. I could go to a progressive dinner at our church—adult company! But what will my children do? It's likely they'll happily languish in front of movies and computer games. I want more for them than this. Impulsively, before I change my mind, I promise to take them to the swimming pool. Not only does this mean I'll miss out on adult conversation, but also it means I'll be wearing a bathing suit *in public,* sinking my always-chilled body into a cold pool, and herding a tribe of my own boys plus their friends through an element created for fish and amphibians. But love not only bids me to squeeze into my bathing suit, love has in fact so schooled my heart that I almost *prefer* this activity over an adult gathering around warm food and conversation with all my clothes on.

I can almost see my childless friends shaking their heads at me, twirling their crazy finger beside their temples. And they are right: this love is a kind of sickness! But it is a sickness that has made me well.

So many others have found the same through their children. Through children who are healthy, feisty, rambunctious, active—and through children who are not. I think of Stanley, the eldest son of dear friends, who lives in a wheelchair, sightless, unable to move or speak. Nearly twenty, he must have his diapers changed, and he is nourished by a feeding tube. His parents and two brothers spend many of their waking hours caring for him.

Stanley's family loves him madly. They find joy in celebrating who he is rather than what he does for them. When I am with them, I am humbled by the unending offices of their love—which are a living tableau of God's own love for us. Here is happiness, then. Not in receiving from our children, but in giving to our children, and so to serve God.

WHAT CHILDREN TEACH US ABOUT WHAT WE'RE WORTH

But there's more: children come to us not just because we desire to love, but also because we need to be taught *how* to love. I saw this dramatized last Christmas at a concert at a special-needs school. I watched high schoolers with autism, Down syndrome, Asperger's, and other disabilities struggle to bring the Christmas message to life. Forgotten punch lines and failed curtain closings characterized the performance, often leaving the actors awkwardly stranded on stage. Most memorable of all, a tall girl in a burgundy velvet dress let loose a spontaneous jig in the middle of the solemn nativity scene, to the delight of the audience. So it went the whole evening, as the gathering of family and friends laughed, applauded, and whistled as if each mistake were a brilliant edit of the original script. And it was. Every mishap was the perfect rendering of each student's uncommon personality.

> Children come to us not just because we desire to love, but also because we need to be taught how to love.

The love in that auditorium of four hundred people was palpable, a hard-won love that had nothing to do with ability, potential, or fulfillment. Halfway through the performance I whispered to my friend Joni, "I don't know whether I should laugh or cry."

She nodded and whispered back, "Our worth is not based on our capacity but on God's purposes."

This brings us to the ultimate answer to the question of why we have children. We read in Romans, "In all things God works for the good of those who love him, who have been called *according to his purpose*" (Romans 8:28). The value of our children is not just about God's purposes for us as their parents. God is using our children to conform us to the image of his Son. Through our children he instructs us, humbles us, and takes us to places of absolute dependence on him. Our children reveal to us what we know we are: beggars before God. But God has clear purposes for our children as well. As we struggle to find meaning in the difficult moments of parenting, God's purpose—a purpose greater than anything our human hands could produce—never falters.

THE PURPOSE OF CHILDREN

We return to the account of Samson, the angel-announced son of Manoah renowned for his mighty strength. Samson's first recorded words stun us. He was now a young man. He wandered down to a town populated by Philistines, the people who had oppressed Israel for many years and were even now the conquerors and enemies of God's people. In his wanderings, Samson saw a beautiful Philistine woman. He returned home and announced to his father, "I have seen a Philistine woman in Timnah; now get her for me as my wife" (Judges 14:2).

These are harsh words. Not only was Samson demanding something of his father, who was supposed to be the respected patriarch of the family, but also the Philistines were uncircumcised, idolatrous people. Samson's demand was a direct violation of God's prohibition against marrying foreigners.

Samson's parents were dismayed. "Isn't there an acceptable woman among your relatives or among all our people?" they asked. "Must you go to the uncircumcised Philistines to get a wife?"

Samson did not hesitate. "Get her for me" (Judges 14:3).

The stories of Samson's life that follow continue on this downward path. They are filled with anger, revenge, violence, and immorality. His wife was burned to death over an altercation with the Philistines. He spent the night with a prostitute. The next woman he lived with—Delilah, another Philistine—was not even his wife. Though she schemed to kill him, he stayed with her, seduced by her beauty. He finally told her the secret of his strength: his long hair.

In that moment of impatience with Delilah, Samson gave away his life. He was captured, his eyes were gouged out, and he was set to grinding meal like an ox. Then he called on God one last time. It was at the Philistines' festival to their god Dagon, which celebrated Dagon's supremacy over Samson's God. Samson asked for one more burst of strength so that he might "get revenge on the Philistines for my two eyes" (Judges 16:28). God granted his request. Filled with supernatural might, he collapsed the temple, killing himself and thousands of Philistines.

This story of Samson and his parents is tragic, with not much comic relief along the way. What was it like for Samson's parents to witness the life and premature death of their son? He had so much potential! Samson was the only man in thousands of years of biblical history with such bodily strength, fueled with nothing less than the Holy Spirit. Yet it seems he accomplished little. What kind of joy could these parents possibly have received from their son? But his story, one of the longest-sustained narratives in the Old Testament, ends with this simple statement: "He had led Israel twenty years" (Judges 16:31). These six words at the end of Samson's life return us to the angel's prophecy before his birth.

Even in Samson's life—a life that began with promise and ended with tragedy—God's purposes were met. As a judge over Israel for two decades, Samson led Israel during difficult years under the Philistines. He was both the symbol and the reality of God's great strength, a living example to the weakened Israelites of what one man empowered by God could do. Though wrong choices, compromise, bad motives, and anger seem to have characterized his life, they are not the whole story. We know this because Samson is listed in the "Hall of Faith" chapter of Hebrews that commends those who "conquered kingdoms, administered justice," and accomplished much for the kingdom of God (Hebrews 11:32–33).

Despite the tragedy here, I find the account filled with great hope for all parents. God did not promise Manoah and his wife joy through their son—though surely they experienced joy at times. But he did promise the deliverance of Israel through Samson, and God did just that. Not even Samson's failures could prevent the accomplishment of God's great purposes.

I am so glad for this God of grace and sovereignty! When a teenager revolts, when a child loses interest in church, even in times of tragedy when a child is hurt or dies, I know nothing else to do but lift my eyes to the Maker of every one of these children, to the God who says of himself:

> I am God, and there is no other;
>   I am God, and there is none like me.
> I make known the end from the beginning,
>   from ancient times, what is still to come.
> I say: My purpose will stand,
>   and I will do all that I please....
> What I have said, that will I bring about;
>   what I have planned, that will I do.
>   (Isaiah 46:9–11)

God's hand reaches from the heavens even to the womb, where one psalmist writes,

> My frame was not hidden from you
>   when I was made in the secret place.

When I was woven together in the depths of the earth,
 your eyes saw my unformed body.
All the days ordained for me
 were written in your book
 before one of them came to be.
   (Psalm 139:15–16)

Manoah and his wife must have laid their hopes and their heartaches for their son Samson at the feet of this all-knowing God. I lay my fears and my ever-changing levels of fulfillment there as well. I am fed by this honey from God, my Rock, who is *this* glorious, *this* trustworthy, *this* sovereign. A God who has knit together every one of my children, who breathes into each the breath of life. As I receive these children, they enlarge my heart, but they are here for even more. They are here to fulfill the purposes of God.

Is Parenting Worth It?

I will not always understand God's plans. I will always struggle to live out my love and faith. Even so, I am awed that I get to be a part of something so vast and significant: the shaping of lives for the purposes of God.

Last week my twelve-year-old son, Elisha, saw his best friend struck by a car. Elisha flew to Andrew's side, took off his coat in the cold morning air to cover him on the ground, knelt by his bloody face to comfort him, and did not leave him until the ambulance drove him away. Elisha's faithfulness to his friend through Andrew's recovery brought me joy, but more, I know that God is purposefully shaping the lives of both boys through this event.

> I am awed that I get to be a part of something so vast and significant: the shaping of lives for the purposes of God.

In so many other occasions in my family's life, large and small, I see God at work. Two summers ago, when we were short-handed in our salmon fishing operation, thirteen-year-old Isaac took on a man's job of skippering his own skiff for the entire season. We were nervous but saw him blossom and mature under the responsibility. Last year Abraham, age six, stood with me in Guatemala as a thief waved a pistol in our faces. We both could have been shot—but God stayed the thief's hand. I listen to and counsel my daughter as she is pulled toward a college major other than the one she has planned for over the last five years. Where is God moving her?

In all of this, in times of challenge, danger, and uncertainty, I return to the God whose promises are sure even when I am not. He *will* accomplish all that he pleases. And all that he pleases will advance the kingdom of God.

Believing these truths releases me from daily weighing the benefits of parenting against the costs. On one side: my daughter's valedictorian speech, my son's sacrificial devotion to a friend, words of adoration from my six-year-old ("You're the best mom I could ever have!"). "Yes! Parenting is *so* worth it!" I announce to all who will listen. On the other side: broken curfews, squabbling sons, a visit from the police, ingratitude. "Forget it! Parenting is so *not* worth it!" I moan to myself.

No longer do my wildly fluctuating levels of fulfillment measure the worth of the whole parenting enterprise, the worth of my own parenting, or the worth of my children. The questions "Is parenting really worth it?" and "Am I fulfilled as a parent?" are, finally, irrelevant. I ask myself instead, "Am I parenting faithfully? Am I parenting consistently? Am I honoring God as I raise my children?" This is what I am responsible for. God is responsible for all the rest. Every day his sure hand is beneath my children, just as it is beneath me.

This is our deepest hope and greatest pleasure. It is a hope that also frees our children as we release from them a weight they were never meant to bear: our expectations that they'll make us happy. Then every moment of delight they bring is extra, grace upon grace, like a jig joyously erupting before a startled audience. We can laugh for days in the unexpected dance.

For Reflection and Discussion

1. What were your expectations of parenthood before you had a child? Where did these expectations come from? In what ways have those expectations been fulfilled? In what ways have they been unmet?

Read Judges 13–14.

2. How does the reaction of Manoah and his wife to the news that they would have a child compare with your reaction when you discovered you would be a parent?

3. What does their story in Judges 13 suggest about their expectations of parenthood?

Read Judges 16.

4. Do you believe God's purposes for Samson were fulfilled? Why or why not?

5. How satisfied with Samson's life would you have been if you were his parent? Why?

6. What does Samson's story suggest about the value God places on a child's life?

7. How might your daily interactions with your child change if you truly believed in God's deeper purposes for your parenting?

Myth 2

Nurturing Your Children Is Natural and Instinctive

Why Biblical Love Is So Difficult to Live Out

Late one night I turned down the hall to tuck in my son Elisha, who was then eleven years old. Thirty minutes earlier, he had literally been climbing the walls, trampolining on the living room couch and chairs, and bounding from one piece of furniture to another in his late-night state of fatigue—despite my warnings, which he ignored. Hearing the ruckus, Duncan came out to discipline Elisha and then sent him to bed.

Planning to make an effort at reconciliation and then have a time of prayer (as was our usual habit), I stepped into Elisha's room and sat beside him on his bed. I began by praising him for his work in the skiff that day. He had driven a skiff full of fish to the delivery boat all by himself—a man's job. After absorbing this compliment, he deftly moved into criticism, challenging a purchase I had made that day: a set of headphones he thought I had paid too much for. I began explaining and defending my decision. An older son came into the room echoing the challenge in a less-than-respectful voice. Neither son would yield his criticism and challenge, nor would I yield my defense. By the time we were done, my heart was cold. I had lost my appetite for sweet affirmations of love and I no longer felt like praying. I got up from Elisha's bed and walked to the door.

"Good night," I spoke coolly from the doorway.

"Aren't you going to pray with me?" Elisha asked.

"No. You pray by yourself tonight." I climbed the stairs, my feet heavy with failure, knowing I should return but not returning.

My life with this son did not begin this way. Do you remember the day your own son or daughter came home? A brand-new being who was now yours. You saw another new being as well: you. You were a parent now, another kind of person. The responsibility was terrifying, yet you had an equally powerful urge to love and protect this little one. His very life depended upon yours—your provision, your touch, your voice. This child now had full claim on you. He would scramble your days and nights mercilessly, leaving you panting with exhaustion at times. Even so, an oozy kind of love would wash over you when you looked at him, propelling you through the intense fatigue. You were not simply the center of this child's world; you *were* his world.

Parenting doesn't always begin this way. Some parents bring a child home and feel overwhelmed by the responsibility, without the assuaging power of immediate love. For them, love grows more slowly, layered day by day, through experience, through the unfolding of the child's personality, through the everyday tasks of feeding, clothing, bathing. A bond is forged over time, until one day—six months later, a year later—the parent knows she deeply loves her child.

And yet this love, whether it comes easy or hard, is not the sunset of the story. I remember the morning my two-year-old daughter shook a defiant fist in my face and said "No!" when asked to take her toys out of the bathtub. I felt a queasy panic. The world—and my stomach—turned.

Once your little one develops a steel will, a vocabulary, and an elevated sense of her place in the world, loving that child can became an Olympic sport. You wake up exhausted every day, all muscles and emotions fatigued, and you realize how very hard you are working to love your son or daughter. The day your son wakes up as an adolescent and comes to the breakfast table dripping with attitude, you know the party's over. The reciprocity—*I love you, you love me back*—has ended.

How can it be so hard to love your child? What happened to the natural instincts God gave parents to nurture their children? Why do you look forward to any chance to escape the house—even a two-hour root canal?

In the next breath, you know the answer. The problem is you, of course. Instantly you prepare the mental list and silently check the boxes down the page:

☑ You're not a good parent.

☑ You're not giving enough.

☑ You're not spending enough time with your kids.

☑ You're not devoted enough.

☑ You're not praying enough.

☑ You're not going to church and reading your Bible enough.

If your guilt is not completely pervasive, a list pops up for your kids as well:

☑ They are not going to church and reading their Bibles enough.

☑ They are strong-willed.

☑ They are selfish.

☑ They are immature.

The problem, obviously, is them!

The truth is, it's all of us. We all are inadequate. But when we conclude our analysis here, we end up spinning in a nonstop centrifuge of guilt and blame. We have forgotten a primary fact: true biblical love is excruciatingly difficult to live out.

WHY IS IT SO HARD TO LOVE?

Biblical love is difficult, if not impossible, to live out because we are sinful, our children are sinful, and we live in a sinful world. Few parents need lengthy arguments to persuade them of this reality. Scripture gives voice to this foundational truth in many places: "There is not a righteous man on earth who does what is right and never sins," the Teacher writes in Ecclesiastes (7:20). "All have sinned and fall short of the glory of God," Paul tells us (Romans 3:23). Our attempts at being righteous on our own, apart from God, are as filthy to him as used rags (Isaiah 64:6). John reminds us, "If we claim to be without sin, we deceive ourselves and the truth is not in us" (1 John 1:8).

Even when we are redeemed, translated from the kingdom of darkness into the kingdom of light, we are never entirely freed from the pull toward trusting in ourselves—our money, our abilities, our decisions—more than God. Even 1 John, the book that unyieldingly commands all believers to a consistent life of love and obedience, also provides for our failures: "If we confess our sins, he is faithful and just and will forgive us our sins and purify us from all unrighteousness" (1 John 1:9). We know that sin so pervades this broken world that all human relationships limp about on less than two good legs. Even the trees and rocks cry out in longing for liberation.

Yet somehow, against the backdrop of Scripture and the reality of life, we have woven images of parental love—especially mother-love—that look like a skip through a lovely park. Our culture depicts a "good mother" as an angel in the house who is naturally sweet, self-denying, and eternally loving. The media create expectations that mother-love, like our culturally formed vision of romantic love, is something you fall into, a delightful sinkhole that leaves you so sated that you don't want to climb out. Parenting models based on the natural mother abound—Intuitive Parenting, Instinctive Parenting, and Primal Mothering, among others. All of these are founded on the premise that mothers know instinctively how to nurture and that "we all really know what our children need," and we can "do what is right for our children by listening to, and acting on, our own parenting instincts."[1] In short, we expect to love our children easily.

For too long our culture and our churches have made light of the life-altering crucibles of pregnancy, childbirth, and parenting. While the motive has often been to affirm parenthood, the effect has ultimately been defeating. It can be *hard* to love our children, because biblical love calls us far beyond our own instincts and abilities. Biblical love challenges us at the very core of our being.

LOVE THAT GOES AGAINST OUR INSTINCTS

When I turn to mothers and fathers in the Scriptures, I see them living out their parental love in far harder circumstances than mine.

Hannah was a childless woman who desperately wanted a son. She prayed that God would grant her this one desire, promising that if he did, she would devote the child to God. God finally gave her the son she prayed for. What joy to hold her son, her only son, for whom she had waited and prayed for so many years! In unbelievable obedience, she returned him to the Lord, leaving her young child to serve at the temple while she went home with empty arms (see 1 Samuel 1:1–2:11).

Moses's mother sent her baby off in a frail basket of reeds upon the river—to die, for all she knew. She believed she would not see him again. But she did. Pharaoh's daughter miraculously hired her as Moses's wet nurse. She nursed him and loved him, the child of her heart returned from the river. And she gave him up again in a few short years to Pharaoh's house (see Exodus 2:1–10). Another death.

David endured the betrayal of his son Absalom, who wanted his father's kingdom more than he wanted his father (see 2 Samuel 13–18).

Zechariah and Elizabeth's childlessness ended with the birth of a boy who would grow up to be John the Baptist. He left his parents and his home to live alone in the desert like an outcast, preaching the divisive news of the coming of God's kingdom. It was a message that would cost him his life (see Matthew 14; Luke 1).

Mary—chosen to conceive, bear, and give birth to the world's only Savior—stood below his cross, sharing in God's agony and devastation.

The Bible is filled with lives displaying the cost of love, the hurt of love, the near impossibility of love. Love that is not returned. Love that must continually give. Love that requires relinquishment of the beloved. Love that is patient and kind and keeps no record of wrong. Love that cuts against all our own instincts.

In fact, nearly every example of love in both testaments is jolting, radical, and unsettling—anything but easy or natural. How hard Jesus's words must have sounded to his followers:

Truly, truly, I say to you, unless a grain of wheat falls into the earth and dies, it remains alone; but if it dies, it bears much fruit. He who loves his life loses it, and he who hates his life in this world will keep it to life eternal. (John 12:24–25, NASB)

If anyone wishes to come after Me, he must deny himself, and take up his cross daily and follow Me. For whoever wishes to save his life will lose it, but whoever loses his life for My sake, he is the one who will save it. (Luke 9:23–24, NASB)

There is no greater love than this, that a man should lay down his life for his friends. (John 15:13, NEB)

I know these Bible passages well. I read them to my children, sing the songs with hand motions. But have I really heard them? Do I see that I am required to fall dying to the ground, to deny my own desires, to lose my life in the name of love? Is this easy? Did Christ speak these words to soothe and placate? In reality these words are a harsh call to an unattainable standard. But here is the incontrovertible truth from Scripture that must be our starting point as we parent our children: *True biblical love is difficult to live out because it is a call to death.*

No wonder as I move toward my angry teenage son in an effort to restore our relationship that I stutter and balk. No wonder I hesitate in offering to take my daughter's place in the fishing boat so she can rest. No wonder I struggled to accept my last two pregnancies. Dying to our own desires and plans is undeniably, excruciatingly difficult.

THE POSSIBLE IMPOSSIBLE

Where does this leave us? Has God locked us into an irre-solvable conundrum in which we are required to use our imperfect hearts to love perfectly our imperfect children in a world that is crooked and bent? Are we required to anni-hilate our very selves in order to lead our children toward life? Jesus spoke to this question in his exchange with a rich young man.

> Our ability to love begins with understanding how radical the call to love is. God calls us to something only he can do in us.

This well-to-do young ruler raced to Jesus and fell on his knees before him. "Good teacher," he asked, "what must I do to inherit eternal life?"

Jesus looked into him and knew that his bank account and extravagant household furnishings were his greatest delight—and his greatest liability. "Go, sell everything you have and give to the poor, and you will have treasure in heaven. Then come, follow me."

The young man was devastated. This was the worst answer possible. He turned away to plod home, full of sadness, "because he had great wealth."

After the young man left, Jesus said to his disciples, "How hard it is to enter the kingdom of God! It is easier for a camel to go through the eye of a needle than for a rich man to enter the kingdom of God."

The disciples were troubled. At that time, wealth was considered a sign of God's approval. They looked at each other, asking, "Who then can be saved?" If even the rich can't get in, who can?

Jesus looked back at them and said calmly, "With man this is impossible, but not with God; all things are possible with God" (Mark 10:17, 21–27).

Jesus's words here are frighteningly honest, but they also bring hope. Listen to what Jesus did not say to his disciples: "What's wrong with you? Why is it so hard for you to give everything up for me? It should be easy and natural. Don't you know it's instinctive to love God first, above all else?"

Jesus, here and elsewhere, said the opposite: the gate is narrow, the road to heaven is hard. By our own strength and will and ability, we cannot get there. So it is with love. No matter how hard we try, we will never get it right every time. We will never love God or one another with perfect love. Only God loves perfectly.

This truth brings immense relief. I am not alone! Love is not hard only for me. True biblical love is difficult for everyone!

Our ability to love begins with understanding how radical the call to love is. God calls us to something only he can do in us. How do we get there? We begin with fear. Recognizing all that God is and all that he requires of us should leave us quaking before him in recognition of his perfection and our deficiency. "The fear of the LORD is the beginning of wisdom," Proverbs 9:10 tells us. Wisdom directs us away from ourselves as the source of ability to God as the source of ability.

The fear of the Lord, then, is also the beginning of love. We can come before his holy throne only because of his great forgiveness. He has erased from the record our selfishness. Through our faith in Christ, he regards us as though we are as pure as Jesus. This is mercy, not justice. This is love, not equity. "How great is the love the Father has lavished on us, that we should be called children of God! And that is what we are!" John wrote with almost disbelieving excitement (1 John 3:1). It is this love, so extravagantly given, that allows me to become a child of God. Standing as the recipient of so much undeserved love and forgiveness allows me to offer the same to my own children. I can love others because God first loved me.

MORE GOOD NEWS

God has done much to move us beyond our frailties, but he offers even more help for the labors of love he bids us to carry out. We are not only given access to the real source of love, but we are also given trustworthy words and enfleshed models to show us how to live out this love. We start with Jesus—God with arms and legs and a lap—who showed us what it looks like to live a God-pleasing life. If we want to see how to live a life of love, we start with the gospels' play-by-play account of Jesus's life.

But even Jesus was not the end of God's provisions. Just before Jesus returned to heaven, he reassured his disciples, "I will ask the Father, and he will give you another Counselor to be with you forever" (John 14:16). God gives us the Holy Spirit as Counselor and Comforter, as a presence within that empowers us to love beyond our own abilities and limitations.

And God offers more: Scripture not only reveals to us the true nature of love, but it also teaches us how to teach our children. We read in Deuteronomy, "Teach [these words of mine] to your children, talking about them when you sit at home and when you walk along the road, when you lie down and when you get up" (11:19). Much of the book of Proverbs is written as a father teaching his son how to live righteously before the Lord. These words are here for us, that we may learn how to love and instruct our sons and daughters.

God also knows our need for living, breathing teachers. Titus tells us how to do this: "Likewise, teach the older women to be reverent in the way they live.... Then they can train the younger women to love their husbands and children, to be self-controlled and pure, to be busy at home, to be kind, and to be subject to their husbands, so that no one will malign the word of God" (2:3–5). How do we learn to love our children and spouses? We learn from others who love well.

There is more. Philippians urges us to fill our minds with "whatever is true...whatever is pure...whatever is admirable..." (4:8). Every one of these virtues is itself a form and expression of love. With discernment, we can find depictions of such love in nearly every media: in literature, music, theater, art, and movies. When we "think about such things," as Paul urges us, our souls are inspired and strengthened in this tenacious work of loving others.

All these resources, both human and divine, provide tangible, incarnated examples that transform God's command to love from a frustrating abstraction to an embodied possibility.

THE COST OF LOVE

One of my favorite movies is *Marvin's Room,* which powerfully presents a biblical view of love. Meryl Streep and Diane Keaton play estranged sisters. Keaton's character has remained single, devoting her life to caring for two invalid relatives. Streep has followed her own desires, marrying, divorcing, moving from man to man. The sisters have been estranged for twenty years when Keaton's diagnosis of cancer draws them together.

In the most poignant scene in the movie, Keaton is gathering the daily doses of pills to take to her dying uncle. Weakened from her own chemotherapy, she spills them. Both sisters kneel on the kitchen floor as they retrieve the medications. As they awkwardly place the pills back on the tray, faces just inches from each other, Keaton reflects, "I've been so lucky.... I've had such love in my life."

> I want to measure love not by what I receive but by the orientation of my own heart and my actions toward others.

Streep is stunned. Her sister, colorless, has never even been with a man; nearly all the love she's known has occurred within the restrictive walls of the invalids' home. "Yes, they love you very much."

"No, that's not what I mean," says Keaton, just a few weeks from her own death. "I've been so lucky to have been able to love someone so much."[2]

I want to say the same of my own life with my children and my husband. That no matter their response to me, my life is rich because I have been able to love *them* so much. I want to measure love not by what I receive but by the orientation of my own heart and my actions toward others.

This last Valentine's Day presented a perfect opportunity for me to express my love for my family. With a glowing face, I set aside my deadlines and ran to the store to gather expensive ingredients. I donned an apron and worked for hours to create an elegant, memorable meal, complete with personalized valentines on each plate. Eagerly, I called everyone to dinner. As they shuffled to the table, the older boys looked at their valentines with embarrassment. Micah, five, didn't like his valentine and began to pout. After we prayed, everyone attacked the food as if in a race. Duncan, surveying my emotional desert, raved about the homemade bread, the salad, the perfectly grilled steak. The boys dutifully mumbled thanks with full mouths, all eyes on the clock—wrestling would soon start. There was no time for the heart-shaped chocolate cheesecake I had made for dessert. In a matter of minutes, everyone was gone—to wrestling and youth group. I stood in the empty kitchen, on a floor littered with carrot peelings, smeared sauce, and radish greens, the counters stacked with dirty dishes, the sink buried under a mound of soiled pans. The leavings of my love feast mocked me. I felt cheated, even bitter. Why doesn't love return measure for measure? What was the point of this? And then I remembered—I wanted to express my love for my family. I smiled ruefully. That is just what I had done.

Sometimes loving others is easy; it is what I want to do. But even in the days when I am immersed in writing about this call to love, I am still falling short. And I always will.

We need to stop pretending that loving our children as God requires is natural and instinctive. No. It's messy. It's arduous. It's costly.

Joseph and Eva Briseno live out this kind of love every day. Their son, Jay, is believed to be the most seriously wounded soldier to survive the Iraq war. Shot in the head at point-blank range, he was not expected to survive his massive injuries. He is blind, quadriplegic, and severely brain damaged. His parents remodeled their house to accommodate Jay's needs, and both quit their jobs to care for their son full time, day and night.

Jay's father says, "If you asked me this from the very beginning, if we can handle it, I wouldn't lie to you. I would say no, that there is no way. There's no way that we're going to learn all these things. But my wife and I, we learned everything. We are the respiratory technician, we are the physical therapists, occupational therapists, speech therapists...his wound care nurse. It's a lot of work and it's hard, and some days are harder than the other days."[3]

The Brisenos openly confess to the hardship, the pain, the brokenness of their dreams. Yet they confess to other emotions as well.

Jay's father explains: "In the basement, every day, [there are] tears, laughter, smiles, pain, fear, hope, faith, name it, everything, love, in the basement. Each moment that Jay can—can share with us, we treasure. God can take him away any time."[4] In a separate interview he noted, "[W]e don't take this as a burden for us because he's our son. We will do everything for him.... We're so lucky to have him. He was a very good son from the very beginning. God gave Jay to us and he's a blessing to us."[5]

Not many of us will be called to this level of sacrificial love for our children, but all of us will work at love all our lives. I continue to fix homemade meals whether it is appreciated or not. Moses's mother continued to nurse her son, knowing he would soon be taken from her. David wished to die in his son's place, even when his son turned against him. Mary lovingly raised the son she knew would someday pierce her heart with sorrow.

Love *will* cost us our lives. If we expect otherwise, we may be tempted to give up along the way. But families like the Brisenos remind us of an equal truth: God's call to an impossible, dying-to-self love is already made possible. The love he calls us to, as hard as it is, is the love he himself unendingly supplies.

For Reflection and Discussion

1. Describe the history of your love for your child. Was it difficult or easy to love him when he first came home? Why? In what ways, if any, has your love changed over the years?

2. Describe a situation in which you felt guilty because it was hard to love your child. How might you have handled the situation differently if you had given yourself the freedom to find loving difficult?

   Read 2 Samuel 15:1–12 and 18:24–33.

3. How does David's relationship with Absalom remind us of how difficult it sometimes can be to love our children? What are some seasons or circumstances in which we might find it difficult to love a child?

4. In what ways does David's love for Absalom expressed in 2 Samuel 18:33 seem more impossible than natural?

5. What does David and Absalom's relationship suggest to us about our relationship with God?

Read John 15:13.

6. In what ways do parents "lay down their lives" for their children? When have you seen this to be true in your own life?

7. What resources does God provide to help you love
   your child even when love doesn't come naturally?
   How could you use those resources the next time you
   find it difficult to love your child?

Parenting Is Your Highest Calling

How Pursuing God First Frees Us to Love Our Children More

Two years ago, after speaking at a conference, I stopped in the reception room for tea. While I gathered some food and drink, a young woman at the table greeted me and congratulated me for speaking so honestly about my two unplanned pregnancies. Another woman, perhaps in her sixties, stood nearby and nodded her head in agreement.

"Thank you," I answered, still warm from the presentation and glad for this appreciative audience. "I really feel called to speak honestly about all it costs to be a mother. We have a tendency—Christian women in particular—to fall back on clichés, to not really acknowledge all that it costs to raise children."

Both women nodded politely.

"How old are your children now?" the younger woman, who looked to be in her twenties, asked.

"My two youngest are three and five; the others are ten, thirteen, and sixteen—and my oldest is going to be eighteen. She'll be leaving for college this spring," I announced wistfully.

"Wow, that's quite a span. My oldest daughter is nine. She said to me the other day, 'Mom, in ten years I'll be leaving for college, living on my own!' I'm glad she's thinking that way, but I thought, *Oh no! Not so fast!*"

The older woman smiled knowingly. "My children are all grown and gone now. Enjoy them while you can."

"I know," the other said. "I can't believe how fast it's going."

"Remember that you're doing good work," the older woman told her. "There will be eternal rewards, and they'll grow up to be such a blessing to you." She smiled encouragingly.

"Yes, I know," the younger woman said. "It's the most important work that we could do. It's definitely the highest calling of our lives."

"Isn't it, though?" the older woman smiled at me, waiting for me to chime in. I smiled and nodded but left the table troubled.

WHAT IS OUR HIGHEST CALLING?

I understand the essence of what these women were saying. I feel it too: my role as a mother to my six children is one of the most essential duties and loves of my life. Yet as I listen to some voices in the Christian culture address issues of family and parenting, I am concerned. Sermons, parenting programs, books, and blogs commonly use the term "highest calling" to describe our role as parents. Many times these words are aimed specifically at mothers. One woman urges readers and fellow mothers to "live our lives to serve our families at our fullest capacity!"[1] I know a number of women who believe their one God-given purpose in life is to be a helper to their husband or a servant to their children. A few Christian organizations issue the same message: God's greatest gift to women is their position as wives and mothers. In addition, many Christian writers understandably link the disintegration of our culture to the breakdown of the family. When the family crumbles, the nation crumbles.[2]

I hear in these words the implication, and sometimes outright declaration, that our work as parents is our greatest contribution to the kingdom of God—perhaps even our *only* contribution. One article lauds mothers in particular for their "service...for mankind and for the kingdom of Christ." By providing a home and godly parenting, "a mother builds something far more magnificent than any cathedral—the dwelling place for an immortal soul."[3]

I hear these messages and tremble, both flattered and flattened by the idea that *my* daily labors at home are building a dwelling place in heaven for my children's immortal souls. That the survival of our nation rests upon my success as a parent. That my performance as a mother will affect the outcome of the entire spiritual war. No wonder I am exhausted and overwhelmed!

This intense spotlight on the home comes to us at this point in our history for good reason. As all of us know, the traditional family is under serious attack. Family units now include same-sex couples and three-parent families in which children's needs are sometimes seen as less important than the rights and whims of adults. Child abuse is rising so fast that it is described as an epidemic by the Child Welfare League of America.[4] As families fracture and states scramble to fill the gap, more and more children are entering foster care. Against the backdrop of such social fragmentation, surely we can assert that our highest call *is* to our families!

But we cannot talk about what is right without turning to the Scriptures. What does God's Word say is the highest call upon our lives? What are we to be consumed with? When we turn from the headlines to the one source of truth (which is also the one source of hope), we find many Bible passages that challenge the assumption that as believing parents our highest calling is to our families.

A MOTHER ON A MISSION

Before he left to face his crucifixion, Jesus gathered the disciples around him and told them what was about to happen. He wanted them to be prepared. He would be betrayed, he told them solemnly. He would be condemned to death, then mocked, flogged, and finally crucified. But on the third day, he assured them, he would rise to life.

The men were not the only ones present during this sacred moment. At least one woman was there as well: the mother of two of the disciples. The next spoken words in the gospel account are hers, and they are a shocking response to all Jesus had just revealed.

"Then"—that is, after Jesus's words—"the mother of Zebedee's sons came to Jesus with her sons and, kneeling down, asked a favor of him."

> "What is it you want?" he asked.
>
> She said, "Grant that one of these two sons of mine may sit at your right and the other at your left in your kingdom."
>
> "You don't know what you are asking," Jesus said to them. "Can you drink the cup I am going to drink?"

"We can," they answered.

Jesus said to them, "You will indeed drink from my cup, but to sit at my right or left is not for me to grant. These places belong to those for whom they have been prepared by my Father."
(Matthew 20:20–23)

I shudder as I read this passage, recognizing myself. This woman's faith was strong. She approved of her sons' new positions as disciples of this radical rabbi.

But this mother came to Jesus not to seek understanding of all he had said. She came not to express her sorrow at Jesus's upcoming sacrifice on her behalf. She came not to marvel at this cataclysmic overturn of human history. She came to Jesus not as a child of God but as a mother on a mission. Her concern was not the death of her Savior but the fame and well-being of her two sons. Blinded by ambition for her sons, she would do anything to secure their future. She asked not simply for a place in the new kingdom for them but for places next to Jesus himself. In her mother's pride, she had elevated her desires for her children above the concerns of the Savior.

Jesus responded with grace to the terrible blindness of this mother and her sons. Rather than castigate them, Jesus explained a truth that ran entirely against their culture, against human nature itself:

Whoever wants to become great among you must be your servant, and whoever wants to be first must be your slave—just as the Son of Man did not come to be served, but to serve, and to give his life as a ransom for many. (Matthew 20:26–28)

I wonder if this mother experienced a burning moment of shame as she recognized the depth of her pride. Perhaps the sting went further—she may have started to reflect on her life as a mother. This might have been a woman who knew a life only of servanthood, acting almost as a slave to her husband's and children's needs and desires. She had buried her own needs and found her fulfillment through the success of her husband and her sons. But what had Jesus just said? That anyone who wants to become great must first become a servant. That Jesus himself came to serve, even to the point of death. And he had come to die for many, not just for his own family. Hearing Jesus's words, perhaps this mother saw that Jesus was calling all believers, women and men, to a life of service that reaches beyond the confines of the home.

Earlier in the gospel of Matthew, Jesus spoke forcefully on this issue, with words that should disquiet all of us:

Anyone who loves his father or mother more than me is not worthy of me; anyone who loves his son or

daughter more than me is not worthy of me; and
anyone who does not take his cross and follow me is
not worthy of me. Whoever finds his life will lose it,
and whoever loses his life *for my sake* will find it.
(Matthew 10:37–39)

The highest call upon our lives today must be the same
call given to the prophets and disciples and believing men
and women throughout history—the same call that came
down from Mount Sinai more than three thousand years
ago, written on stone tablets with the finger of God. What
does God require of us above all else? "You shall have no
other gods before me" (Exodus 20:3). In the New Testament,
Jesus said, "Love the Lord your God with all your heart and
with all your soul and with all your strength and with all
your mind" (Luke 10:27).

We *know* this, don't we? The question is, how do we live
this out in our homes? How do we negotiate this call with
other passages that tell us to love our husbands and children,
to honor our mothers and fathers, and to love our neighbors
as ourselves (Titus 2:4; Deuteronomy 5:16; Matthew 19:19)?

I believe this commandment comes to us first not only
because it reflects the most essential truth about God—that
he is the One and Only—but also because our greatest and
most constant temptation as parents is to unseat the Sovereign from his throne and replace him with our family. We

may reason that as long as we do not replace God with ourselves, as long as the God substitutes are God-given—our children and spouse—and we are *serving* and *loving* them, as God commands, then this must be good and acceptable!

But God's love is frighteningly exclusive. "Do not worship any other god, for the LORD, whose name is Jealous, is a jealous God," he proclaimed to Israel over and over (Exodus 34:14). Despite the clarity of these words, few heeded them at the time—at great cost

> Our greatest and most constant temptation as parents is to unseat the Sovereign from his throne and replace him with our family.

to themselves. But one ancestor, Abraham, fully obeyed this command with startling results.

We know the outline of Abraham's story already. If we turn to it again with parenting eyes and hearts wide open, we will be ushered deep into the heart of God, into his holy and jealous love, and into his expectations for us as parents.

GOD'S TERRIFYING CALL

When Abraham received the most terrifying call any parent can imagine, he was already a man of great faith. Yet God asked him for more—nothing less than the life of his son. God's phrasing of his demand tells us that he knew what this would cost Abraham. "Take your son, your only son, Isaac, whom you love," God said, "and go to the region of Moriah. Sacrifice him there as a burnt offering" (Genesis 22:2).

Abraham received this call from God not just as a father but as a certain *kind* of father—a man who had waited twenty-five years for God's promise of a son to be fulfilled. No one had greater cause to love his child than Abraham. He had received no promises from God for any more sons after Isaac. If the sacrifice were carried out, Abraham would not only lose his son but also would have to live with the knowledge that he was the slaughterer of his own son. And he was to slay Isaac upon behest of God—the giver of all life and the giver of this particular, promised life.

How easy was it for Abraham to trudge up the mountain with a knife in his hand, fingering the blade on his belt as he watched innocent Isaac tread up the steep slopes, carrying the wood for his burning on his own back? Abraham could have said no to this God. He could have loved his son so passionately that he refused. His wife's happiness, all his hopes of future lineage, their desire for grandchildren, the joys of raising a child—all this could have wooed him from a God he had never seen or touched. It would have been the most fatherly, natural thing in the world for Abraham to say, "No, I will not give up the son I love and hold and sing to at night for an invisible God. I will not give up this miracle child who came from God himself." He could have said no out of his concern for God's own promises that "through Isaac...your offspring will be reckoned" (Genesis 21:12). For all these reasons, or even just one of them, Abraham could have chosen the life of his son over obedience to God.

But he did not. Instead, he sacrificed his son to God that day. He bound him in ropes, laid him on the altar, and raised his arm for the strike. Isaac was as good as dead. Hadn't Abraham rehearsed this moment over and over in his mind as he climbed the mountain? We know this because the book of Hebrews tells us that he believed God could raise Isaac from death (Hebrews 11:19). And in a sense, God did. Just before the killing blow descended, God spoke again and stayed Abraham's hand. God sent a ram to take Isaac's place—a ram that foreshadowed the coming of Christ as the sacrifice that takes our own place in judgment. What God asks of us, he himself will provide.

As he returned down the mountain, with his son running ahead and the weight of impending death now gloriously lifted, Abraham had a deeper understanding of God. He keeps all his promises in the ways that *he* chooses. As a man of faith, Abraham was revived and strengthened. He was certain to love God more.

After choosing obedience to God over his love for his son, what kind of father did Abraham become? I am certain he did not love his son any less. But perhaps his love changed. He was now freed from requiring from Isaac what only God could give. His legacy was not his blood-and-flesh progeny but his extraordinary faith in God, which God counted as righteousness (see Galatians 3:6). Then, because Abraham loved God above all else, God extended his fatherhood, making him not just the father of one son but the father of "many nations," the father of all of us who claim the blood of the Lamb foreshadowed that day on Mount Moriah (see Genesis 17:4). All of this makes clear that God's family is birthed, not through bloodlines and genetics and marriages, but through God's adoption of us as his sons and daughters.

Is It Possible to Serve Our Families Too Exclusively?

Does God require of us what he required of Abraham? We are seldom presented with this kind of agonizing choice to make clear the highest call upon our lives. Yet we can't leave this narrative tucked away in the pages of our Old Testament. Abraham's story speaks across more than three millennia into our own homes and families.

It *is* possible to love our children too much. I think of Mae, a woman I met in Canada a few years ago, who abandoned the church when her daughter declared herself a lesbian. Mae, however misguided, believed she had to make a choice between retaining her daughter's love and retaining her belief in the authority of the Scriptures. She chose her daughter.

It *is* possible to love and serve our family too exclusively, to believe that in serving them we are fulfilling all that God asks of us. If we have numerous children, or even just one with particularly demanding needs, our family and household concerns will indeed occupy us for most of our lives. But a hungry world of need waits outside our doors. Yes, God calls us to our own family, but he also calls us to the highway where a stranger from another family, ethnicity, and religion lies bleeding, a stranger whom God calls our "neighbor" and commands us to love.

> It *is* possible to love and serve our family too exclusively, to believe that in serving them we are fulfilling all that God asks of us.

The family reunion that awaits us at the end of time is not a reunion with our family of origin or the family we are raising but a reunion with God our true Father and our blood-bought brothers and sisters. In heaven God will commend his faithful people with the words "Well done, good and faithful servant" (Matthew 25:23), not "Well done, good and faithful parent."

Never are we to forget that the children we have are given to us by God. They are here to serve him and fulfill his purposes. And out of all the loves possible in our lives, out of all the calls upon us, we must pursue the highest call: "You shall have no other gods before me"(Exodus 20:3; Deuteronomy 5:7). God calls us to an exclusive love for him that consumes our hearts, souls, minds—all that we are.

This might mean giving up the idea that we alone are the best and only godly influence upon our children. It might mean that we hire a baby-sitter in the afternoon so we can spend uninterrupted time in Scripture or serve at a food bank. I think of my friend Brian, a father of three, who travels to Honduras for two weeks every year to work at a health clinic he founded. For me, serving God means that I will spend some of my hours at home in front of the computer writing, instead of spending that time with my family, as I obey one of the callings God has placed on my life.

I cannot tell all the ways our love for God can be expressed in the context of a hurting world. It is for each of us to find means of service within the world and lives we are given. I do know that parenting is indeed a high calling, an awesome privilege. Some of the happiest moments of my life, the taste of heaven, come when my children are gathered around the table, their faces like flowers. I know the joys of working together in our family-owned commercial fishing operation, all of us bound in a common pursuit. I know the gladness of seeing my children serve the Lord. But I know an even greater call: the call to know and love God.

FREED TO LOVE MY CHILDREN RIGHTLY

If I pursue God first as my highest call and am satisfied in his love, then I am freed not to love my children less but to love them rightly. I am freed from the error of the disciples' mother, who sought identity and signif- icance through her sons rather than in her role as God's redeemed daughter. Like Abraham, I discover

> If I pursue God first as my highest call and am satisfied in his love, then I am freed not to love my children less but to love them rightly.

that God's promises are rooted in God alone, not in my chil- dren or any other person.

Knowing this, when my children disappoint me, I need not be shaken. I am freed to love them as God loves them— not because he craves their attention, not because he needs them to need him, not for what they will bring to him or do for him, but simply because they are *his* and he desires to pour out his love upon them.

We are asked to lose our lives in Christ's life, not in our children's lives. Our greatest faith and highest hopes are not in our daughters and sons but in the Son who has already come.

For Reflection and Discussion

1. What are some of the callings on your life right now? When are you most likely to feel those callings compete with one another?

2. Do you believe it's possible to love your child too much? Why or why not?

Read Genesis 22:1–19.

3. What do God's words in verse 2 suggest about how God sees our relationship with our children?

4. How did God use Abraham's obedience to bless the nation of Israel (see verses 15–18)?

5. In what way(s) might Abraham's obedience to God have freed him to love Isaac more?

6. When are you most tempted to put family before God?

7. Describe a time you experienced God's blessing on your choice to serve him before directly serving your family.

8. What practical changes might you need to make this
   week in order to put your calling to God before your
   calling to your family?

Myth 4

Good Parenting Leads to
Happy Children

Exchanging Shallow Hopes
for God's Deeper Purposes

The boys and I were in Chicago, standing by the trunk of a car I had just rented. We were about to leave on a day trip. The trunk was so clean and inviting, like a hobbit hole, that three of them crawled inside and cozied up together, laughing and jostling.

"Mom, can we ride in the trunk on our trip today?" Isaac, age fourteen, asked from the trunk.

"That would be fun, wouldn't it?" I smiled, glad for their creativity and their desire to be together.

"Please? Can we?" begged Abraham and Micah, four and six, now leaping out with excitement.

"Look, there's plenty of room!" my fourteen-year-old called from the corner of the trunk.

He was serious? I craned my neck and peered into the recess at his face.

"What's wrong with riding back here?" he asked again, eyes wide with innocence.

"Get back in, Abraham and Micah!" the fourteen-year-old called. "See, we can fit! It's perfectly safe, Mom!" Three of them now were laid out like sausages, each one begging as if for bread. "Please, Mom, please?"

Still disbelieving, I took a breath and asked in what I considered an admirably controlled tone, "Okay, just for clarification, you want to ride back there in total darkness, squished, with the top locked down and no escape, where you'll breathe in exhaust, instead of riding inside the car on a comfortable seat, breathing oxygen, where you can see where you're going?"

"Yeah! Yeah, Mom!" they chorused, somehow taking hope from these words.

"And look, we don't even need seat belts!"

I did resist the temptation to grant the boys' ridiculous request, but I can't claim the same fortitude in every situation—after all, most decisions are not so simple. The decision that took us to Chicago and dozens of other destinations that year was agonizing. Duncan and I had planned for years to take the kids out of school for a year and travel or live overseas. Finally the right time had come. Naphtali was in her first year of college. Isaac, who had skipped seventh grade, would catch up to his peers by sitting out the year. We told the boys about the trip a year in advance to give them time to adjust to the idea.

Upon first—and second and third—hearings, the boys were upset, as we expected and understood. They would leave behind all that was familiar on our Alaskan island, where they had lived all their lives, and step into the unknown.

During that entire year of preparation, the boys worried aloud and tried to change our minds. We responded to their questions patiently, with good humor, but the boys' displeasure gnawed at us. We believed we were doing what was in their best interest. We wanted them to appreciate the vastness of God's world. We wanted to pull away from other influences and focus on one another and the people and places we would visit for this one year. But I questioned myself constantly. How could this be right and good for our family if it made them all unhappy? Would good parents do this? At the heart of my disquietude was the presumption that good, godly, and effective parenting could be measured, at least in part, by the happiness levels of my children.

How Much Are My Hopes for My Children Really Hopes for Myself?

We all want our children to be happy. This desire is not unspiritual or wrong, but sometimes it has an underside. In the pursuit of our children's happiness we can engage in all kinds of dubious activities as parents. Up to one-half of American children have televisions in their rooms despite evidence that it erodes study habits and sleep.[1] Many parents go into debt to provide "the best" for their children, reports *Smart-Money* in the article "Parents Gone Wild (for Their Kids)."[2] Each child has to have his own bedroom; birthday parties become increasingly extravagant, with rented ponies and carnival rides. One study concluded that a key factor behind most family debt is the "elevated lifestyles" parents are attempting to provide for their children.[3]

> I wonder how much of my hopes for my children's happiness are hopes for myself. If my children are happy, then my parenting life is quieter and less complicated.

Here is my own confession. I wonder how much of my hopes for my children's happiness are hopes for myself. If my children are happy, then my parenting life is quieter and less complicated. I find myself falling into this trap more often than I wish. A prime example: for Isaac's thirteenth birthday, we agreed to a sleepover party. I braced myself for this massive boy fest. Six more boys added to my five, which meant charges up and down the stairs, flying objects, lots of shouting, and possibly the destruction of furniture. I wanted to be right there in the nucleus of it all—the fun mom, presiding over the riot with the lavish dispensing of Cheetos, party honkers, and Band-Aids as needed.

But when Isaac's friends showed up at the door, they arrived with armfuls of electronic games. My brave party face and my mother's heart sank. My first instinct was to tell them to march their gaming stuff back to the cars. I wanted them to be boys, to play in the world of oxygen and matter, exercising their real bodies with Nerf balls and footballs rather than twitching their fingers to move cartoons on a glass screen. But my second thought was different: *Hooray, I'm saved! They'll all sit in the family room attached to the television, the house will be quiet, and I can get some work done.* And that's what happened. They were plugged in, motionless and happily anesthetized for most of the evening. I was happily in my office, working on this book, freed from my usual duties of crowd control, conflict resolution, activities directing, and relationship building with my sons' friends. I let the gadgets take my place.

We're all guilty of sometimes choosing the lesser good of convenience and immediate gratification over the higher good of being present for our children. We don't need to beat ourselves up about this every time; sometimes we just need a break. But sometimes there's more behind our attempts to satisfy our children.

DOES GOD WANT OUR CHILDREN TO BE HAPPY ALL THE TIME?

Without any chapter and verse justification, I have blithely assumed that if I do everything right my children will be content. I have made the same assumption that Elihu made more than three thousand years ago. Elihu was the youngest of the "friends" who came to talk with Job after he'd lost everything. Elihu appeared last in the book and cast himself as "one perfect in knowledge" (Job 36:4). In one of his many arguments against Job, he claimed that "if they [men] obey and serve him, they will spend the rest of their days in prosperity and their years in contentment" (Job 36:11). There it is! My own supposition (shared with many I know in the church) goes like this: *If we obey God, God will bless us here and now, and we'll lead wonderful, prosperous, and joy-filled lives all our days.* The special parenting version of this beguiling principle is this: *If we parents obey and serve God, then our children will grow up happy, and we will spend the rest of our lives in prosperity and contentment.*

I *want* this to be true. I want to live in prosperity and contentment. But God rejected this formulaic theology, along with the words of Job's other friends, who advanced similar arguments. The sovereign Lord rebuked them all, saying, "You have not spoken of me what is right" (Job 42:7). God did not provide an alternative formula or explanation for Job's suffering. He simply appeared in all of his majesty, omnipotence, and authority and silenced the men's attempt to reduce him to simplistic and self-serving equations.

So does God want our children happy all of the time? In the article "The Principle of Nurture," the author assures us that "God wants children to be happy. Happiness is part of the blessing God wants for our children.... When we provide the right kind of nurture...we can and should expect both happy and obedient children."[4] Some writers go further and regard happiness as the primary measure of a child's spirituality and obedience. One popular and controversial writer even teaches that God *requires* children to be positive and happy all the time, including when being disciplined. "A cheerful, compliant spirit is the norm. Anything else is a sign of trouble," he warns, advocating discipline for any outward expressions of displeasure.[5] I have overheard Christian parents chastising young children for not evidencing cheer, though the children had just lost a treasured possession or were not able to go to the park as they had hoped.

If God's first concern for his children is their happiness, then many stories in the Bible need to be rewritten. Let's follow just one story, that of the Israelites, whom God called "a child" and "my son" (Hosea 11:1). Consider how this story would read if God's first desire for his child was happiness.

The new pharaoh pressed the Hebrew people into slavery. Their piteous cries rose to their Father's ear, and he mourned for them, his heart breaking to see them so abused. When the time was right, their Father planned for their release from slavery. God did indeed deliver them powerfully!

But the way out of Egypt into the desert was difficult. The people grew hungry and tired as they journeyed. They sat upon the ground one day, longing for food. "If only we were back in Egypt! We had plenty to eat there." God the Father, hearing his children's complaints, was saddened that they doubted his ability to feed them. He ordered Moses to pack up the tents and head back to Egypt.

The Israelites returned to Pharaoh, who was delighted to enslave them again. As they wearied in the mud, making bricks once more, the Israelites cried to their Father again. He grieved again for their misery and planned once more to liberate them...

Other narratives would have unfolded differently as well.

God disciplined the Israelites for refusing to believe his promises—they were to wander in the desert for forty years. But after a year, God got tired of hearing complaints. Every day they grumbled about the manna, sweetened bread from heaven that he showered upon them. This punishment was God's punishment as well. Thirty-nine more years of this!

Their dissatisfaction wore him out. God called off the wandering and announced they could enter the Promised Land next week. They weren't ready yet, of course. They were still immature and idolatrous, but he knew they would be so much happier.

What would have happened as they settled into the land?

The children of Israel had settled in the land God the Father had given them, a land as full of milk and honey, wine and wheat, as God had promised them. But they soon disobeyed God's commands and took wives from among the surrounding nations and built temples to Baal on every mountainside.

God knew that the hardness of their hearts required drastic intervention or they would be lost forever. His instrument would be the army of Babylon, who would conquer the city and all its inhabitants.

But as the army approached Jerusalem and the Israelites' cries of fear rose to his ears, God winced. At the last moment, he turned the army back. The people in the city shouted for joy at this miraculous deliverance. God's heart warmed at their joy.

But they were praising Baal, not God! They believed Baal had saved them from the enemy.

God was grieved at their blindness and rebellion, but his Father's heart could not bear to see the suffering he knew it would take to restore his children to himself. He would leave them as they were.

No, no, and no. All of this reads as blasphemy. God's first concern is always his children's holiness, not their happiness. Without understanding this, we will never understand how God could allow his children to endure four hundred years of slavery and then sentence them to forty years of desert wanderings. We won't understand how David could cry out in agony, "How long will you hide your face from me?" (Psalm 13:1). And we won't understand why he allows our own suffering today.

GOD PARENTS FOR HOLINESS, NOT HAPPINESS

We hear little of holiness these days. We live in what David Wells has called a "therapeutic culture," in which we favor relationships over morality. If we were to ask our fellow churchgoers to choose the attribute that most defines God, most would speak of his love. And God's love for us is indeed a precious truth. We do well to teach our children "Jesus Loves Me" as their first Bible song. But Wells is right when he charges contemporary Christians with believing that "God is centrally love and that He is only peripherally and remotely holy."[6]

In emphasizing God's love over his holiness—his set-apartness as a sovereign, omniscient authority—we end up believing that his central concern is our individual happiness. I heard a radio speaker the other night announce with great assurance that "God is our coach, our best friend. He is on our team, like a cheerleader, cheering us onward." In a sense this is true. But is God on our team, or are we on God's team? Have we replaced God's holy robes of righteousness with a cheerleader's jumpsuit? The book of Hebrews reminds us that we are to worship God with reverence and fear because "our 'God is a consuming fire'" (12:28–29). God's holiness is not simply one attribute among many. Holiness permeates his very being. As Wells warns, without some understanding of the holiness of God, "our faith loses its meaning entirely."[7]

Our faith will fail, too, if we forget that God requires *us* to be holy. "Be holy because I, the LORD your God, am holy," God commanded us in the Old Testament (Leviticus 19:2). We, too, are to be set apart. Jesus spoke the same in the New Testament when he called us to be perfect (Matthew 5:48). Sin and holiness are such grave matters that Jesus spoke these hard words: "If your right eye causes you to sin, gouge it out and throw it away. It is better for you to lose one part of your body than for your whole body to be thrown into hell"

(Matthew 5:29). To get rid of sin, be ruthless, spare nothing, he tells us through hyperbole. Our own purity and righteousness are that important, for "without holiness no one will see the Lord" (Hebrews 12:14).

No wonder Jesus did not turn from the agony of the cross, nor did the Father. Without Jesus's death on our behalf, we would never see God. We could attain holiness no other way but through his covering of our sin, his blood in place of ours. But Jesus did not die as some kind of masochistic act. Hebrews tells us Jesus endured the cross for the "joy set before him" (Hebrews 12:2). His joy was to secure our holiness! And here is the beginning of our answer.

WE DON'T NEED TO CHOOSE BETWEEN HOLINESS AND HAPPINESS

Holiness and happiness are not exclusive states. One is not of the flesh and the other of the spirit, though Hollywood might tell us otherwise. When did you last see anyone on the big screen attempting to be holy while also having a good time? The "holy" are usually depicted as simple-minded, corrupt, and colorless. Heaven is often shown as a place of boredom, where angels sit around on puffy clouds strumming harps absent-mindedly.

Our vision of holiness is so narrow. In truth, *holiness is the way to happiness.* When we are finally purged from our sin, we will find no higher joy than the presence of our God and Father, whose unfolding omnipotence and beauty will enthrall us for the rest of time and beyond.

This is what I learn as a parent from these breathtaking truths. Yes, I am aiming for my children's happiness, but it's a certain kind of happiness. The happiness that comes from standing before the Sovereign One without guilt or fault because of Christ's redemption. The

> Our vision of holiness is so narrow. In truth, *holiness is the way to happiness.*

happiness that comes from knowing and delighting in God. The happiness that carries us through shadowed valleys and poverty and death and loss, because God goes with us. None of this precludes the happiness that comes from amusement parks, hikes in the forest, and birthday parties. Last winter I went with my three older boys on a zip-line tour of the rain forest in northern Guatemala. Two hundred feet off the ground, in the rain. We had a blast together. God delights in our fun. But an essential question guides even these activities: How can I move my children toward holiness and happiness in God?

Asking this question led me to a familiar and powerful passage of Scripture that I suddenly saw with new eyes. In the Beatitudes we find that holiness and happiness are beautifully and inextricably blended.

BLESSED ARE THE BROKEN

It was the early days of Jesus's ministry. He had just called James and John from their fishing boat. Now he was walking throughout Galilee, "teaching in their synagogues, preaching the good news of the kingdom, and healing every disease and sickness among the people." From all over Syria, people brought to him "all who were ill with various diseases, those suffering severe pain, the demon-possessed, those having seizures, and the paralyzed, and he healed them" (Matthew 4:23–24). Huge crowds from Galilee, Jerusalem, and Judea, and even the region across the Jordan River followed this God-man who could restore with a single touch. Can you see them leaping to their feet and running exuberantly to their families—whole, healed, fully themselves?

When the last had been touched and made well, when the cries of celebration had died down, Jesus led the crowd of thousands up a mountainside. Every eye, every ear—all now open and well—was fixed upon this one who had brought more joy in those hours than anyone had ever experienced or expected.

But the first words Jesus spoke must have shocked them. He spoke about blessing. Yes, they knew about that now—hadn't they just received it? But then he said, *Blessed are those who are poor in spirit*—not happy are those who are healed. *Blessed are those who mourn*—not happy are those who rejoice. *Blessed are those who hunger and thirst for righteousness*—not happy are those who are fed and satisfied. *Blessed are the meek*—not happy are the powerful. *Blessed are those who are persecuted*—not happy are those who are comfortable (see Matthew 5:3–12).

This is what blessing looks like, Jesus told them. It's not simply different from what we think; it is the opposite of what we think. And he told us why. When you are spiritually poor instead of self-satisfied, you are blessed because God gives his kingdom to the needy. When you mourn over your sin, you are blessed because God will cover your sins. When your longing for God's righteousness is as tangible as physical hunger and thirst, you are blessed because you will see God's righteousness revealed. The merciful will receive mercy. The persecuted will be rulers in God's kingdom.

Some of these rewards may come to us now, at least in part, simply by anticipating their coming fulfillment. All will be made well and whole. But that is not our condition at the moment. The most blessed among us are not those who are fully satisfied, content, and spiritually self-sustaining, but those who are broken, who want, who need, who long for what is promised.

BLESSING BEFORE HAPPINESS

All of this changes how I think about my responsibility to my children. Instead of hoping for their happiness now, I hope for their blessing. It is not possible, nor even desirable, to raise my children without any want or need or unhappiness. Even if I did all that I can as a Christian parent—even if I were *that* good—there would still be holes in my children's lives, places for God to fill and heal.

This doesn't mean that now I have a blueprint that magically eases my daily decisions. Should I allow my son to go to the prom? Do I let my twelve-year-old buy an iPod? Should I make my son attend Sunday school if he doesn't want to go? I struggle with all these questions as I try to shift my focus from my children's mercurial levels of happiness toward deeper questions. I am asking, how can I parent in such a way that my children hunger and thirst for righteousness? How can I parent in a way that steers them toward mercy rather than equity, toward meekness rather than dominance, toward mourning rather than partying? How can I parent in such a way that they are rocked free from their peers' obsessions with here-and-now gratification?

> It is not possible, nor even desirable, to raise my children without any want or need or unhappiness.

I have made a few small starts. When Elisha was ten, I took him with me to the funeral of a friend's baby who had died of SIDS. He did not want to go, but I knew he needed to see mourning. When my four older children were small, we made fifty to one hundred sandwiches every month for a homeless shelter. Every day of every summer, my children spend most of their waking hours out on the open ocean pulling fish from the nets, whether they are excited about it or not, because it is our family's work and they are needed. When my children's grandmother died tragically, I did not shield them entirely from the circumstances of her death. They needed to feel grief and sorrow, even anger, before I rushed on to the good news of her presence in heaven. And we did take that trip last year—uprooting our family for eight months, leaving safety and predictability behind for a greater good.

I am learning that it does not serve my children's good to attempt to fulfill all their desires—most of which are not about pursuing God but about pursuing other things. Nor is it my job to try to shield them from all of life's injustices or from the consequences of their decisions: getting cut from a sports team, failing a crucial exam, losing homework and winter coats, forgetting lunches every other day. My kids might need to go hungry once in a while, just as I need to feel hunger. They might have to give something up, just as I do at times, to sacrifice for others, to go where they may not want to go. Only then will they—and I—be prepared to live out our faith in the world.

PARENTING IN THE WIND

My sister-in-law once planted a young Japanese maple in her yard. Concerned about the wind (she lives on a stormy ocean-front), she placed the tree behind the house, in a quiet, pro-tected corner. The tree grew gorgeous purple leaves that summer and the next, but by the second autumn, it began to sag, straining against the stakes and wires she had stabilized it with. Finally the tree collapsed in the grass beside her house. She suspected voles at first, but when she related the tree's condition to the nursery owner, he asked where she had planted it. When she told him, he said, "The tree is too pro-tected. It needs the wind to strengthen its fibers. It needs the wind to make it strong."

It is possible to spend ourselves in the labor of preserving our children's happiness only to have them grow up weak, unable to withstand life, seeking their immediate happiness over lasting holiness and blessing.

I don't want my children to topple. I want to help them grow tonicity and strength, like the tree in Psalm 1. That tree is firmly rooted in the banks of a gushing, living stream. Its leaves never wither. It yields bright, bursting fruit through every season of its life. I pray that we can love our children enough to parent them toward *this* kind of happiness!

For Reflection and Discussion

1. What outside voices pressure you to parent for your child's immediate happiness?

2. What thoughts and emotions do you experience when your child is unhappy?

3. Describe a time in your own life when God parented you for the sake of your holiness, beyond your desire for immediate happiness. How did you react at the time? What are your reflections about that situation now?

Read 1 John 4:16 and Hebrews 12:14, 28–29.

4. In what ways have you seen God's love emphasized to the exclusion of his holiness, perhaps even in your own life?

5. In God's relationship with us, are these two character-istics—love and holiness—mutually exclusive or inter-dependent? Explain your answer.

Read Matthew 5:1–10.

6. Consider each blessing in verses 3–10. How are these blessings similar or different from how you usually hope and pray for your child?

7. Consider each promise given in verses 3–10. How are these promises similar to or different from what you want for your child?

8. In what circumstances do you find it most tempting to parent for your child's happiness rather than for her holiness?

9. What is one practical way you can parent for your child's blessing rather than for her immediate happiness this week?

If You Find Parenting Difficult, You Must Not Be Following the Right Plan

Learning to Rely on God Rather Than Formulas

The night I first knew we'd finally have a family was the night Duncan almost died.

He was traveling on a fishing boat to Kodiak. Near midnight, he was gently rolling side to side in his bunk, asleep. It was blowing that night, with sloppy seas. The boat began to move sluggishly in the waves with a slight list. Soon the deck was awash. Duncan was shouted awake, and he and the two others on board pulled on their survival suits and abandoned ship in the dark—just moments before the boat sank.

That same night, after a long flight from Alaska to New Hampshire, I faced another kind of excitement. The trip had been more exhausting than usual and my period was late. On the way to my mother's house from the airport, I ducked into a late-night drugstore and bought a home pregnancy test, trying not to hope. After ten years of marriage, after nearly two years of trying to conceive, after several rounds of infertility testing and many negative pregnancy tests, this time the pregnancy test stick turned color—a solid pink line. I lay awake much of that night, curled around a minuscule glob of cells that I knew were furiously multiplying into something that we would call our son or daughter. I could hardly express my joy, and I couldn't wait to tell Duncan the news.

The phone rang at my mother's house in New Hampshire at nine the next morning. "Duncan's on the line!" my mother called to me. Why was he calling at five in the morning, Alaska time? What was he doing up so early? His voice was shaky as he greeted me, and then all I heard was sobbing. Soon I was sobbing with him. It could have turned out so differently. How many did we know who hadn't been rescued, who didn't get off their boats in time, who didn't have a boat nearby to find them before it was too late?

This is how parenting began for me—in the shadow of near death, teaching me already how precious and how precarious are the comings and goings of life. When we brought our daughter home from the hospital, the storms were over, I thought: the storm of longing for a child, the storm that almost left this new baby fatherless, the storm of a long, hard delivery. Awash in hormones, aswim in ignorance, floating with elation, I was sure the hardest part was over.

Just the Beginning

In some ways, I was right. That fierce longing for a child was now at rest. But in other ways, my naiveté was laughable. It didn't take long to discover my ignorance. The decisions and turmoil began with a simple question the first night our daughter was home: where should she sleep? Should she sleep in bed with us at night, transforming the marriage bed into the family bed, or should she sleep in her own crib? That, of course, was only the beginning of parenting dilemmas, all of which felt weighty and possibly life altering. Should I breastfeed only or supplement with a bottle? Should I feed her on her schedule or on mine? Should she sleep on her back, her side, or her stomach?

As the months and years passed and more children entered the family, the questions only multiplied. How soon should we discipline, and then *how* should we discipline—spankings, time-outs, removal of treats, or some combination of all three? Did I dare leave them with a baby-sitter, and if so, for how long? Or should I stay with my children at all times? How much of our mainstream culture would we let in the door? What about education: public school, Christian school, or home school? Should our teenagers have curfews, and if so, what time? Behind every question was the same question all parents ask: How do I raise this precious child well? More than that, how do I raise her in the "nurture and admonition of the Lord" (Ephesians 6:4, KJV)?

Overwhelmed and unsure of myself, I took to books, radio shows, and online materials, searching for insights, practical solutions, and discipline techniques—anything to simplify a job that was rewarding but also far harder and more complex than I had ever imagined. I discovered that the joke universally told about new babies—that pocket-sized cameras arrive with operating manuals but new human beings arrive with none—is not true. Manuals and child-operating instructions abound—shelves of them, all promising answers to every dilemma and question. Many boast best-selling status and post huge sales. Some of the most popular books offer more than parental advice; they promise nothing less than instructions in raising children as God himself would.

Intrigued, tempted, and alarmed all at once, I began to look at some of these manuals and materials more closely. I found a clear divide in approaches to child rearing. On one side were writers and parents who emphasized the authority of the parents over the child and focused on his inherent sin nature. Because of the stamp of original sin, a child's cries are considered manipulative rather than communicative. One book, under the heading "Never Too Young to Train," instructs the reader to begin training with her newborn. When a newborn cries as he or she is being set in the crib, "the battle for control has begun," the author warns ominously. "Crying in order to manipulate [the adults] into constant servitude should never be rewarded."[1] The same writer provides directions for spanking sessions, including descriptions of the length and thickness of the switch, adjusted for each age, and the process to carry out the procedure.

This and other books teach that the parent should direct feeding as well. One immensely popular book, with sales in the millions, advocates that the mother nurse the baby according to her own schedule rather than the baby's needs. This parent-directed scheduling, ideally, also trains the baby to sleep through the night in a matter of weeks.[2]

In a parent-centered approach, discipline and authority are central concerns. I read parenting writers who claimed that training children was as simple as training dogs[3] or training roses.[4] A mother of ten who writes online parenting materials compares raising children to growing and staking out tomatoes.[5] For her, as for other writers, instant obedience is the key to raising godly children.[6] In this model, the home is to be spiritually pure, a fortress or bulwark against the secular culture. Separation from all potentially negative influences is the key to spiritual growth and purity.

On the other side, across the divide, I found writers and parents advocating a child-centered approach in which the parents conform their lives and schedules to the child's needs. In this model, often called attachment parenting, mothers breast-feed as long as possible, "wear" their babies to keep them close, and establish deep bonds with their child. Co-sleeping in the family bed is encouraged—the needs of the child always come first. Discipline matters are less prescribed and spanking is less popular, if not completely avoided. Great care is taken to preserve the esteem of the child. Parents are encouraged to follow their God-given instincts.

I have read materials on both sides, comprehensive materials that issue guidance from the moment of birth until the child leaves home. Both claim to be biblical and both summon Scripture to support their views. Each side has drawn hundreds of thousands of passionate adherents worldwide who testify to the success of the system, saying such things as "This book changed my life. My child is happy and healthy because of this book." And each has acquired detractors who issue dark warnings about the same book, accusing the writers of fanaticism and abuse. At least two of these books have sparked nearly a thousand online reviews each.[7]

I understand the emotional energy underlying these debates. Every writer and reader and parent wants to do the best for her child, to bring her up in the most God-honoring way possible. But how do we find our way among competing child-rearing philosophies, all of which claim to be biblical?

THE PLAN GOD USES

To answer this question, I have to return to the Scriptures rather than delve further into the parenting literature. What does God tell us about raising our children? My goal is to find and read every verse in the Old and New Testaments, in context, that speaks to the raising of children. Most of these are the same verses used in Christian parenting manuals. Here is what I find:

- In Genesis, God commanded Abraham to teach his children and his household to "keep the way of the LORD" (Genesis 18:19).
- Four verses in Exodus instruct parents to teach their children about the Passover, God's mighty deliverance of his people from Egypt (see Exodus 12:26–27; 13:8, 14).
- The sixth commandment God gave to his newly redeemed people was for sons and daughters: "Honor your father and your mother, so that you may live long in the land the LORD your God is giving you" (Exodus 20:12).

- Deuteronomy 21:18–21 instructs parents to take hold of a rebellious son who will not respond to their discipline and bring him to the elders at the city gate, where he is to be stoned to death.
- Five verses in Proverbs advise the use of a "rod" as a means of correcting a child, driving away foolishness, shame, and the danger of hell (see Proverbs 13:24; 22:15; 23:13–14; 29:15).
- Another verse in Proverbs speaks of the importance of disciplining a son (see Proverbs 19:18).
- The first nine chapters of Proverbs present the words of a father teaching his son how to obey the Lord and avoid sin.
- Proverbs 22:6 urges us to "train up a child in the way he should go" (KJV).
- In several places in the Psalms, the psalmist vowed to teach his children the fear of the Lord (examples: Psalm 34:11; 78:4–6).
- Jesus said nothing specifically about child-rearing methods, but he spoke powerfully of the immeasurable value of children: "The kingdom of God belongs to such as these," and "Anyone who will not receive the kingdom of God like a little child will never enter it" (Luke 18:16–17). He warned that anyone who causes a child to sin is better off drowning in the sea (see Matthew 18:6).

- Jesus redefined and enlarged the family on two occasions, warning that "anyone who loves his father or mother more than me is not worthy of me; anyone who loves his son or daughter more than me is not worthy of me" (Matthew 10:37). He also said that his "brother and sister and mother" were not determined by blood but by "whoever does God's will" (Mark 3:35).
- Ephesians 6:1–4 provides teaching for both children and parents. Children are to "obey your parents in the Lord." Fathers are not to frustrate their children but are to "bring them up in the training and instruction of the Lord."
- Colossians repeats the command for children to obey their parents (see Colossians 3:20).
- Titus 2:3–4 admonishes older women to teach younger women to "love their husbands and children."

I am grateful for every word from the Lord on children and parenting. I believe his Word is sufficient. More than sufficient—abundant! I come away from this search with a renewed commitment to teach my children the ways of the Lord. Clearly we will be accountable to God for this. But I confess that this exercise shocked me as well: the Bible includes very few verses about raising children. In fact, I find far more verses on the treatment of skin diseases than the treatment of children (but I'll spare you a catalog of those!).

Where are the instructions on feeding, sleeping, specific discipline and training methodologies, God's chosen means of education—all the issues and philosophies that parenting writers have addressed with such certainty, claiming biblical authority? God does not appear to indulge us on this front.

Neither did God indulge anxious parents in the Scriptures. Here we cast the biblical net wider, beyond the specific verses on child rearing. We know God *must* have more in his Word for us as parents. And he does.

Why Us?

As I consider the many biblical narratives that focus on families, I realize our biblical forebears must have struggled with the same question that preoccupies us today: How do I raise my child in a God-honoring way?

Imagine one step further. Imagine how it felt to be the parents of miracle children, children who arrived through direct divine intervention and astonishing angelic pronouncement! God announced to Abraham and Sarah that they would bear a child in their elderly years, a son who would himself be the father of nations. Elizabeth and Zechariah, also elderly and childless, were visited by an angel promising a son who would "make ready a people prepared for the Lord"

(Luke 1:17). Mary and Joseph, who were expecting a wedding, not a child, were told by the angel Gabriel that their son would "be called the Son of the Most High" (Luke 1:32).

All these parents-to-be must have been overcome with joy. But on the heels of such joy there surely came great fear and anxiety: *A son! A son is coming to us. But why us? How could we have been chosen? What do we know of raising a special child from God? How can we do this?*

One of the biblical narratives gives us that fuller story. We return to the story of Manoah and his wife, told in chapter 1 of this book. The angel appeared to Mrs. Manoah with the news that she would conceive and have a son and that he was to be a Nazirite, "set apart to God from birth." When she delivered this message to her husband, he must have been as incredulous and exuberant as she was. But his first words upon hearing the news reveal not joy but humility and fear—a recognition of his sin and inexperience. He fell to his knees and prayed, "O LORD, I *beg* you, let the man of God you sent to us come again to teach us how to bring up the boy who is to be born" (Judges 13:8).

Can you hear Manoah's heart? His fear of parenting badly, of not doing as God wished? His understanding of the magnitude of this mission God had given? He accepted the assignment, but he begged God to teach him how to fulfill it.

God heard this fervent prayer and sent the angel again. (Such compassion for terrified parents-to-be!) Manoah approached the angel respectfully, asking the one question that plagued him through his sleep, through his waking days: "When your words are fulfilled, what is to be the rule for the boy's life and work?" (Judges 13:12). In other words: What do I do? Give me some direction, some rules, some guidelines, some kind of program!

But the angel did not respond to this question as Manoah hoped. In fact, he did not respond to this question at all. He did not give parenting advice or rules or methodologies or philosophies. Instead, he merely repeated what he had told the woman at their first meeting: "Your wife must do all that I have told her. She must not eat anything that comes from the grapevine, nor drink any wine or other fermented drink nor eat anything unclean. She must do everything I have commanded her" (Judges 13:13–14).

Manoah and his wife must have been puzzled and disappointed. He asked for help in parenting and instead received a few rules for his wife's eating and drinking. Perhaps this was comforting in some ways. But it still did not seem to address their need for parenting instructions.

God's Silence and Our Attempts to Fill It

Here it is again: silence from God when we want answers! Even biblical narratives leave us feeling empty-handed. In the face of more silence than most parents want, many writers have attempted to fill in the spaces, responding to our needs and insecurities with clear directives. Often these are cobbled-together versions of pragmatism and behaviorism, lists of prohibitions, and specific tricks that worked with the writers' own children, buttressed by a few selected Bible verses.

I once heard a two-part radio series on the biblical roles of husbands, wives, and children built around a single verse: "Your wife will be like a fruitful vine within your house; your sons will be like olive shoots around your table" (Psalm 128:3). Entire books with detailed discipline systems and lists of rules have been constructed out of an often misunderstood verse in Proverbs: "Train up a child in the way he should go: and when he is old, he will not depart from it" (22:6, KJV).

We all want so badly to do it right! We build entire rule structures around one verse taken out of context. Our desire is so strong that it even tempts us to reach outside the bounds of Scripture to fashion a model for raising godly children.

Dr. Tim Kimmel, in his book *Why Christian Kids Rebel,* reminds us that the Bible does not prescribe a single model of child rearing:

> There is no set biblical way for children to behave or dress or talk or play. God has called us to create an environment for our children where they can get a clear sense of the love, forgiveness, and grace of God.

On top of that, He has given us the mandate to build qualities like respect, honor, decency, fairness, and modesty into the core of their character.

God allows children a lot of latitude in how they live out their personality type within the boundaries of these wonderful values. God is too much into original thoughts and ideas to create some mold that produces the "perfect Christian kid."[8]

As we raise our children, we can trust God's Word in every way. His Word is complete and his Word is sufficient—in all that it addresses and all that it does not.

PARENTING IS MORE ABOUT PEOPLE THAN PROCESS

When we shift our perspective from the outward to the inward, from rules to relationship, our parenting will change. In his manifesto, "Solving the Crisis in Homeschooling," pastor Reb Bradley wrote with admirable vulnerability about his conversion from prescriptive-based parenting to relationship-based parenting. Bradley and his wife, the parents of six children, always took parenting seriously. They read countless books, watched shelves of videos, listened to as many tapes as they could. "We wanted to do whatever it took to get results with our children," he writes. But they made a serious error, he confesses: "We majored on the 'process,' and as we gleaned new techniques we would stir them into the parenting mix, subjecting our children to it." There was lots of love and affection in the home, he writes, "but we had the wrong idea of what it meant to have influential heart relationships. We loved our kids, but who they were as people was inconsequential to our process.... I had yet to learn that fruitful parenting is more about *people* than *process.*"[9]

I am learning this as well. Now, I am not opposed to process. Didn't I potty-train most of my children using a minutely prescribed (and gloriously successful) Pavlovian-style toilet-training method? Wasn't I the one who went about crowing with pride at my own additions to the process? (If you reward with M&Ms, you can teach colors, counting, and bladder control all at the same time—presto!) I, too, wish for processes and programs that will simplify this maddeningly messy and individualized challenge of parenting. I, too, want eight hours of sleep, time for myself, all the perks that come to the pilot of a tightly run ship. I, too, access books, online materials, advice from friends to help me through. But as I grow as a parent, I am learning to resist the urge to rely on systems and formulas; I am learning to mistrust claims of a single biblical model for parenting. I can give up this search because God has given something more.

WHAT GOD WANTS MOST

I am beginning to understand the final words given to Manoah and his wife. When they pleaded for instructions on how to raise the coming deliverer of Israel, the angel did give them rules—not for the boy's life but for their own. Instead of listing specific parenting strategies, the angel addressed something much larger: the orientation of their hearts. Every moment that Mrs. Manoah ate and drank, and all the hours spent in preparing to eat and drink, she had to choose to surrender and obey the Lord's commands rather than her own appetites and desires. And though the prescriptions came to the mother, they were not to her alone. These commands influenced Manoah's hunting practices, his choice of meat, and how their food was prepared every day. It would require both parents to keep the angel's instructions.

> Godly parenting begins not in the rules we or other people make for our children but in pursuing a genuine relationship with God.

The given instructions would, paradoxically and perhaps unexpectedly, complicate their lives rather than simplify them.

Here, then, is how God prepared this couple for parenting: by calling them into a deep, daily, costly dependent relationship with himself. So it is throughout the Old Testament.

God provided explicit rules for his people, such as the Ten Commandments, the instructions for feasts and for sacrifices, and provisions for the forgiveness of sin. But these laws were never meant to be ends in themselves. They were always intended as means of knowing God, learning about his holiness, and entering into relationship with him. "A man is not justified by observing the law.... So the law was put in charge to lead us to Christ" (Galatians 2:16; 3:24).

When the rules are followed as external behaviors in themselves, separated from a genuine relationship with God, perversion always results. God snorted in disgust as his people went through the motions of offering sacrifices to him. "Do I eat the flesh of bulls or drink the blood of goats?... These people come near to me with their mouth and honor me with their lips, but their hearts are far from me" (Psalm 50:13; Isaiah 29:13).

This is what God wants most from all of us: our hearts. Godly parenting begins not in the rules we or other people make for our children but in pursuing a genuine relationship with God. We cannot parent our children in God's ways unless we know God as our own loving parent. Knowing God and depending on him is the beginning of godly parenting.

This means that my first steps as a parent are like my first steps taken as a child: they are taken on my knees. I have been there—hands open, crying, praising, pleading for wisdom, like Manoah before the angel. I am still there now. The hardest and the most real work of parenting is done when I give up my own agenda and seek God's, when my heart asks to be molded to God's will and character. If I want my children to be conformed to the image of Christ, I must seek to be conformed to Christ first.

God has already shown us the way. He parents, not according to an external list of rules, but according to his nature. Because he is a God of abounding love, he showers love and tenderness upon his children. Because he is a God of clarity and fairness, he provides definitive expectations for his children. Because he is a God of justice, he punishes his children's sin. Because he is a God of truth, who always fulfills his word, he disciplines their violations just as he promised. Because he is a God of mercy, he makes a way for their sins to be covered. Because he is a God of hope, he offers restoration even in the midst of judgment.

The gospel we teach most effectively is the one that we embody and walk out before our children, not the gospel that trips easily off our tongue. Our children learn less from the rules we outline or the programs we follow than from the lives we live before them.

CHOOSING AMONG PARENTING MODELS

So how do we choose among competing parenting models? The answer is, we don't have to choose among models at all!

Instead, we need to choose to give up the notion that God has given us a comprehensive child-raising rule book and that his primary concern is that we do everything "right." Pursuing our relationship with God before anything else frees us to see each child in her own uniqueness rather than squeezing our children into a prefabricated mold. It frees us from the expectation of total control. It frees us from unbiblical promises of sure outcomes. It frees us from seeing our children as products rather than people.

At the root of all of this, we need to choose to give up the quest for an expedient parenting life. The only perfect parent—God himself—led a parenting life that was anything but expedient. His relationship with his son Israel was mercurial, thorny, time-consuming, and consistently inconvenient. We know why. The Old Testament reminds us of the truth all parents live with every day: every child arrives as a fearfully and wonderfully made creation with a steely will and heart and mind bent toward serving self. Considering our children's ability to make choices, their God-given uniqueness, and their sin-damaged hearts, how can we reduce parenting to an efficient one-size-fits-all program that will make life "easy"?

The most quoted parenting verse in Scripture—one sometimes used to create those one-size-fits-all programs—actually steers us in the opposite direction. "Train up a child in the way he should go: and when he is old, he will not depart from it" (Proverbs 22:6, KJV) is written in the singular rather than the plural. "Train up *a child* in the way *he* should go," rather than "Train up all children in the way they all should go." The writer points us away from a systemized kind of parenting and toward a personal, individualized relationship that requires a deep understanding of each child and his particular God-shaped nature.

All of this takes time—so much more time than most of us realized it would. Ironically, once children come along, our tasks and need for efficiency drastically multiply, yet what children need most from us is not our speed and dispatch but our time, our calm, our presence. With six children, these are my scarcest resources! I am one of the original Speed Queens, an obsessive multitasker, born with a hyperactive internal clock. After my fourth child was born, I dispensed with the tock part of the ticktock—who needs that extra time-wasting beat? It is a daily struggle for me to set aside this task orientation, to slow down, to ignore the household and professional work that constantly calls to me. But God gives me grace to remember that raising children is not a task to accomplish or an item on a to-do list. What my children need most from me is my time and my presence—and that's what God desires most from me as well.

If we still find ourselves tempted to fall back on parenting programs, efficient formulas and prescriptions, a danger awaits. It is easy to transfer our trust and our dependence

from God to the systems themselves, even to the creators of
those systems. Worse, we can transfer our faith in God to
faith in our own ability to implement the system successfully.
Pastor Bradley has seen this pattern repeatedly.

> I have heard from too many parents who feel like
> failures, and they are especially baffled as they list all
> that they did or didn't do: *no TV, no videos, no video
> games, no dating, no bad music, no youth group, no
> institutional church, no neighborhood friends; they
> homeschooled, dressed modestly, groomed conservatively,
> memorized the Scriptures, and baked their own bread.*
> They were intensely dedicated to rearing their children
> for God, but their trust was not really in God alone—
> it was in what they did for God.[10]

The recognition that God does not sanction one particular methodology of raising children may sound like bad
news at first, but it brings enormous freedom. I can listen to
others' experience and advice. I can peruse parenting books
for ideas. I can glean the good from every source. But I needn't
be tied to any single program. God's Word gives me much
more freedom than that. I nursed all my babies on their own
schedules most of the time. In a few short seasons, as needed,
I nursed them or gave them a bottle on my schedule. When

my two-and-a-half-year-old son kept failing the potty-training method that all my others passed with banners and flags, I put away the book. It didn't work for him. I did not discipline all of my children the same way, despite some manuals' insistence. Some needed spanking; others needed only a word or a look. My older children have advanced to running their own fishing boat, not by prescribed and preordained rules, but by their own maturity level and desire. I am freed to let my relationship with each child develop organically, within the unique context of our personalities and our home. I am freed to trust myself more than third-party experts who know neither me nor my child. Most of all, I am freed to trust God.

FINDING FREEDOM

Recently a group of parents from my church met at a retreat. We talked about family rules and habits and the realities of our lives with our spouses and children. On the outside, we looked like a fairly homogeneous group of Christians, yet as we talked openly, it soon became clear that our parenting styles were wildly varied. On the topics of movies, Sunday dinners, church attendance, family meals, employment, discipline techniques, and education, we represented a variety of choices. As I listened to each person, stories bubbled up from every corner.

Jody's son, who is autistic, has just learned to sit through an entire church service. "He takes off his socks and shoes during the sermon, strewing them over and under the pews, but that's okay. At least he's quiet!" Jody smiles.

"My kids fall asleep on me in church almost every week," Michelle announces. "I let them. I can't be poking them awake every minute."

> No other parent or writer, no matter how many books they sell, no matter how many children they have raised, can know our children as God does or as we do.

"I know all the books say we're supposed to eat dinner together, our whole family," Questa adds. "But it works out much better with my husband's schedule for us to eat before he gets home."

"My son can handle only one instruction at a time. I see other kids following a lot more steps, but I'm finally learning just to tell Wes one thing and then follow through," says Liz.

We laughed together and shared sympathy and suggestions as we opened our parenting lives to one another. Among the eight of us, we had thirty-five kids—each one with distinct challenges and needs. Needs that kept some up every night. Needs that required special time and patience.

In those moments of grace, I realized anew that parenting is not a project or an experiment. Books and programs and prescriptions do not raise children. No other parent or writer, no matter how many books they sell, no matter how many children they have raised, can know our children as God does or as we do.

This knowledge frees us to parent like God—not according to a human-sourced formula but according to love and knowledge, not according to ease and efficiency but according to individual needs. Our relationship with each one of our children can be as living and dynamic as our own relationship with our heavenly Father. He loves us freely, irrationally, and according to his nature, and we are to love our children the same, regardless of inconvenience and cost. We can celebrate this freedom and rejoice in God's inexhaustible creativity, poured out in every child he has given. And poured out upon us as we parent in the footsteps of our Father.

For Reflection and Discussion

1. What are some areas of parenting in which you have attempted to follow a particular methodology? What did you find most helpful and least helpful about following that plan?

2. Consider a difficult behavioral issue you're dealing with in your household right now. Do you believe God prescribes one particular method of handling that situation? Why or why not?

Read Ephesians 6:4.

3. In what ways can the advice of others help you to bring up your child "in the training and instruction of the Lord"?

4. In what ways can overreliance on one parenting plan or piece of advice "exasperate" your child—and you?

Read Proverbs 22:6.

5. How might this verse free you to parent according to your individual child's needs?

6. What are some distinctives you've learned about your child's needs and personality that help guide you in knowing "the way he should go"?

7. When have you adjusted a parenting plan because it wasn't meeting the needs of your child? What was the result?

8. How does the knowledge that God parents according to his particular relationship with each child bring freedom to your parenting? In what ways is God's heavenly parenting inefficient?

9. How could you respond, verbally and/or internally, the next time you feel pressure to follow a particular parenting plan as the "right" way to handle a situation with your child?

You Represent Jesus
to Your Children

How We Trap Ourselves in a Role
We Weren't Meant to Play

March 2002. At 7:00 a.m. the radio coughs awake. "Thank you for joining us on this broadcast! We'll be looking at God's role in…" I knew three hours ago how hard it would be to get up this morning. Micah had two feedings in the night instead of one. Abraham was up with a bad dream. Since I am on night duty with the kids, Duncan usually takes the morning shift and lets me rest, but he is traveling this week.

I lie under the blankets, listening to the perky radio voices in the room, waiting for motivation to coalesce in my weary body. A new broadcast, then a song: "I want to be your hands; I want to be your feet…" I recognize it as one of my favorite current songs, by Audio Adrenaline. With my head still on my pillow, my eyes closed, I whisper the words softly, addressing them to Jesus, "I'll go where you send me; I'll go where you send me." I know where I have been sent and where I must go in about five minutes: into each of the kids' bedrooms, calling each one awake, my hands helping theirs in buttoning their shirts, pulling on socks. Four need to get ready for school, while the youngest two will stay home with me.

I believe that I am the hands and feet of Jesus to my children. How many sermons have I heard on this? "We are to be Jesus to our children. We are the first Jesus our children know." It's a familiar and beautiful message to me. Micah, four months old, cannot feed himself. He waits for me to dress him, to change his diapers. His very life rests in the care of my hands for most of each day. Abraham, just over two, toddles after me everywhere I go, imitating my every move. The older four all try to commandeer their own lives but still need me in important ways.

I sing through the final words of the song, grateful for this start to my day. I am lifted up. This is the day I am going to do it right. All of it, I vow. I am going to be Jesus to these little ones. "Whatever you did for one of the least of these brothers of mine, you did for me," Jesus told us (Matthew 25:40). This is the same Jesus who wrapped a towel around his waist and bent to the floor to wash his disciples' filthy feet—feet that he himself had shaped. The God of the world on his knees in its dirt.

I can do this. Cut my children's toenails, wash their dirty bottoms, cook their breakfast, drive them to school, send them off with a kiss and a prayer. Whoever would be exalted must humble himself. Let the day begin!

But nothing happens as I intend. The extra ten minutes I took to get up as I considered these things have cut us all short. Breakfast is burned; Elisha can't find his homework; Isaac and Noah are fighting; Micah cries in the swing, hungry because he didn't get fed all of his banana. I develop a massive headache and can't give the kids the attention each needs. Two of the boys fight—vigorously—on the way to school. I shout at them and threaten to pull over.

By the time I deliver the four kids to the school parking lot, I have stopped singing the song in my head.

What happened to the hands and feet of Jesus? I wondered on the drive home. I saw him for about a half hour. I was the tender mother spooning mashed bananas into her infant's pursed mouth. The mother who offered good morning hugs to all. The mother who lovingly lined up the bread for sandwiches, remembering who likes mustard and who hates mayonnaise. But then Jesus's hands and feet started swatting, and his tongue launched a few sarcastic remarks. By the time the car was loaded and the kids arrived at school, it definitely wasn't Jesus behind the wheel! What happened? How did I lapse—again?

Why Can't I Be Like Jesus?

When I think of Jesus at such times, I see him surrounded by mobs of desperate, sick, crippled people. Not six of them, but six hundred, even six thousand, sitting on a hillside in utter ignorance—and hunger. Jesus satisfied them all, the bread and fish multiplying in his hands, his words speaking such truth the crowds were transfixed. Then mobs thronged him wherever he went, asking for healing, mercy, justice. Hands outstretched to him, pleading, begging, and demanding.

In my own tiny way, I have a sense of what this feels like. Uncountable needs and hurts surround me. I desire to attend to each one with kindness, compassion, and discerning judgment that metes out exactly what is needed. I want to heal what is broken, right all wrongs, establish the kingdom of God here, in the hearts of my children, within the walls of my home. I want to be a smiling, white-robed figure moving through the needy people with gentleness and authority.

One of my favorite pastor theologians teaches that parents are to demonstrate to their children what it means to have God as a parent. He urges mothers and fathers to take their roles seriously, because...

the most fundamental task of a mother and father is to show God to the children. Children know their parents before they know God. This is a huge responsibility and should cause every parent to be desperate for God-like transformation.... Will the child be able to recognize God for who he really is in his authority and love and justice because mom and dad have together shown the child what God is like.[1]

I want desperately to do this, but I am not sure I am capable of parenting in such a way that my children see God through me. My well of sympathy goes dry; my healing touch hardens. By early evening, I am longing only for rest and healing myself.

Is this idea wrong, then? Not completely. Not only are we the spiritual body of Christ, but also, God tells us, in some mysterious way we are the physical body of Christ. This is a healthy corrective to a kind of Gnosticism that dogs Christianity, denying any goodness in the material world. I welcome this perspective that attends to bodies as well as to souls. As people of faith, we do not simply proclaim the gospel on the street cor-

> We live out the gospel in our own bodies as we take the message to the streets and hospitals and then to the hardest place on earth: our homes.

ners, relying on our words to announce the good news. Nor do we sit and fold our hands all day long in isolated contemplation. We live out the gospel in our own bodies as we take the message to the streets and hospitals and then to the hardest place on earth: our homes. Rather than disembodying our faith, "we are to become Jesus on earth.... We are to serve like Christ, love like Christ, live like Christ, be like Christ," as a recent sermon reminded me.[2]

But this truth can be distorted, taking us to two opposite extremes: to an exaggeration of spiritual authority and omniscience or to a crippling, unbiblical, and imbalanced servitude. As parents, we can be tempted in either direction.

THE TEMPTATION TOWARD AN UNBIBLICAL AUTHORITY

Theologian Karl Barth warned more than forty years ago against the dangers of believing that "parents should feel and act towards their children as God's representatives."[3] It is possible to take on the mantle of Jesus with too much confidence. It is possible to invest so much spiritual authority and power in ourselves as parents that we believe it is *our* efforts that create Christlike character in our children.

One writer compares children to warm chocolate and the home in which they're raised as the mold. "Melted chocolate hardens into whatever shape it is dispensed into.... If I pour the chocolate purposefully into a God-shaped mould I will have helped make something worth raving about."[4]

Another writer, in his essay "The Majesty of Mother-hood," tells us that it is the mother, not the father, whose emotions establish "the condition of the entire household." Echoing the teachings of psychologists in the 1970s, he warns that children's minds are like video recorders, registering every word, gesture, expression, and even tone of the mother's com-munications. "And all of it contributes to the person he will become.... His [the child's] emotional pattern is set by the time he is two years old. That should be a sobering realization to mothers."[5] Mothers, then, are singularly responsible for who their children become.

But do we accomplish the "character of Jesus Christ" in our children's lives, or does Christ do this? Are we empower-ing ourselves with an authority that belongs to Christ alone?

If we misunderstand the idea that we are the hands and feet of Jesus to our children, we slip further into error. We can assume a kind of omniscience over our children. We can believe that we are capable of seeing into their hearts and minds, and then we treat them according to our assumptions.

One popular and controversial writing team advises par-ents to be "on guard to discern attitudes." They tell us that our child's external compliance isn't enough—we must look into the child's heart and guard it, for the heart is the root of all evil. When children are young and are not yet able to "keep" their hearts, that job is entrusted to the parents. Parents are to discipline not just for actions but also for attitudes, which the parent can discern by keeping a close watch on body language, facial expression, and other telltale signs of unhappiness or rebellion.[6]

Certainly the point that sin starts in the heart is biblical, but children can become the enemy in this model. The doctrine of original sin can be so emphasized that even infants must be disciplined from the beginning by the knowing, redeemed parent. One writer cites Psalm 58:3 in support of this idea: "Even from birth the wicked go astray; from the womb they are wayward and speak lies." Parents are warned against a baby's manipulations, her false representations of need: the need for milk, for snuggling and for physical contact. The infant's sinful desire is to "gain excessive indulgences." Physical punishment, administered by the parent, is a means of removing sin from a child's heart.[7] The parent, in all cases, is expected to have full understanding and control over his children.

WE CANNOT BE JESUS; WE CAN ONLY NEED JESUS

How does this view of parenting measure up to Scripture? While the disciples tried to send the children off with stern commands, Jesus invited the children to his side. He held them and blessed them rather than rebuking and controlling them. In fact, Jesus told us that if we want to enter God's kingdom we must become like little children ourselves, for "of such is the kingdom of heaven" (Matthew 18:2–4; 19:14–15, KJV). Jesus's words are refreshingly radical. What could be more countercultural than to aspire to the dependence of a child rather than the authority of an adult?

The call in the Scriptures to imitate Jesus moves us in the same direction. I am convinced that the Bible's command to "be like Christ" was not meant to empower us but to humble us. In the face of that call to perfection, we confront our own sin and discover the most essential piece of news we need to know about ourselves as parents: we are weak, fallible, and desperately in need of grace.

I experience this daily, recognizing again and again that rather than *being* Jesus, I am *needing* Jesus. And this realization has been my deliverance. I fail in my efforts to be Jesus to my children because I am *not* Jesus. My children came to that conclusion far sooner than I did! Nor am I any kind of savior. I am a sinner saved by grace, and I will continue to be that until I stand in God's presence, whole, perfected, my redemption finally and fully accomplished.

> We never replace Jesus in our children's lives. We don't even do the work of Jesus in our children's lives. We do the work of parents, which is to point our children to Jesus.

We never replace Jesus in our children's lives. We don't even do the work of Jesus in our children's lives. We do the work of parents, which is to point our children to Jesus. And then Jesus does his own work—with or without us. It is not Jesus's authority and omniscience that we are called to imitate but his humility, his servanthood, and his sacrifice. In this way alone are we his hands and his feet in our households.

THE TEMPTATION TO SERVE TOO MUCH

And so the call to imitate Christ ushers all of us into servanthood rather than authority. Jesus "did not come to be served, but to serve, and to give his life as a ransom for many" (Matthew 20:28). He took on "the very nature of a servant" (Philippians 2:7). *This* is how we represent Jesus to our children. Paul wrote to the Galatian church, "You, my brothers, were called to be free. But do not use your freedom to indulge the sinful nature; rather, serve one another in love" (Galatians 5:13). Peter urged the early Christians to "live as free men, but do not use your freedom as a cover-up for evil; live as servants of God" (1 Peter 2:16).

I know many parents who are beautiful and fruitful servants of Christ in their own homes. I hear women in particular encouraging one another onward in this goal. One woman writes on her blog, "No matter what we do at church, in ministry, or on the job, we get one chance with our families to serve them unconditionally and when I don't feel appreciated for what I do, I remember God gave [my husband and kids] to me to serve."[8]

But even in this biblical mission of servanthood we can fall into imbalance. The Scripture verses on the previous page were all written or spoken by men—Jesus, Paul, and Peter. And many verses on servanthood directly address men in particular. Yet many of us assume that servanthood is a woman's domain alone. We fall into the trap of believing that authority is the realm of men, while servanthood is the realm of women, especially mothers.

One verse in particular has fed this tendency. "Wives, submit to your husbands as to the Lord," Paul taught in Ephesians. We forget that men are called to more than submission: "Husbands, love your wives, just as Christ loved the church and gave himself up for her" (Ephesians 5:22–25). Men are called to a love ready to sacrifice to the point of death.

I know numbers of women who "do it all": care for the children, the house, and their husbands. Some add to this a job outside the home to support the family. As I listen to mothers online, to private lives made public through chat rooms and blogs, a common thread twines among them, whether they are single mothers, whether they work at home, work outside the home, homeschool, or do any combination of the above: fatigue. One woman who homeschools multiple children and helps to run a family business writes sadly in her blog that she must give up her last bastion of self—her thirty-minute daily nap. But she will do it, believing God is calling her to this further sacrifice.

Many mothers express their desire to serve their families like Christ and spend many hours every day doing just that. But they constantly struggle with guilt—they are not doing enough. And then they feel guilt for their fatigue and lack of joy. I am one of these women. I fall into bed at night remembering not the good I did that day, but all I did not do.

In our desire to be the hands and feet of Jesus to our children and family, is it possible for us to serve them in such a way that other biblical admonitions are ignored? It is indeed. Luke's story of two sisters illustrates exactly this.

A TALE OF TWO SERVANTS

We know the story well. Two sisters were in their home in the village of Bethany, about two miles from Jerusalem. Jesus and his disciples were traveling through, and Martha opened her home to them. Her invitation was a gracious act of hospitality that revealed her heart, but the preparations for a meal for at least thirteen hungry men were daunting. How would she feed all those appetites? It's not that the men were coming soon for a meal—they were already there waiting for the meal. What pressure!

Martha began her frantic preparations immediately, but Mary did not join her sister's work as she normally did. She stayed in the room with Jesus and the men and found an open spot directly at the rabbi's feet. This was a bold act of faith that countered the Jewish tradition of segregating genders during worship and teaching. But Jesus allowed her that position. Imagine how excited Mary must have been.

Martha, however, was less than thrilled. Didn't Mary know that it was the woman's role to serve men? How could Martha do all this alone? When she could no longer contain her anger, she complained to Jesus, knowing he'd tell Mary to get in the kitchen, where she belonged.

I am sure Martha felt justified in these complaints. She had heard of all the ways Jesus himself continually served and healed others. She knew that Jesus called everyone to serve. Yet his response stunned her.

"Martha, Martha," Jesus said to her. He saw into her heart—it wasn't hard. Her heart was written all over her anxious face. "You are worried and upset about many things." Jesus looked into her fretful eyes. "Only one thing is needed."

Martha must have frozen in her steps. What was the one thing? Wasn't it just what she was doing? How could anything else matter at this moment but serving Jesus?

But Jesus continued, "Mary has chosen what is better, and it will not be taken away from her" (Luke 10:38–42).

Martha's service—considered women's work in her culture and still in ours—would indeed be "taken away," leaving only dirty dishes and a messy kitchen. But Mary's absorption of Jesus's words and presence would sustain her throughout her life.

What is sometimes better than serving Jesus? Attending to the words of God.

How did Jesus know how much women needed to hear this? I know I am a Martha. I am pressed on all sides to give, to serve, to fix healthy meals, to deliver goods to those who need them. I am surrounded by needs, as every parent is. How many women are like me, running and working and serving until we are hollow-eyed, too tired for the Word of God, too fatigued to sit at the feet of God each day with ears and eyes attuned to truth? How many of us try to be the hands and feet of Jesus until we're nearly too exhausted to feed ourselves? Jesus encourages us to feed ourselves, to sit quietly at his feet, to let go of our household duties for a time in favor of something better.

Jesus illustrated this higher value again with another woman. He had just dramatically driven a demon from a possessed man. Following this exorcism, one woman in the crowd, moved and stirred by his miraculous powers and his authoritative teaching, called out loudly above the crowd, "Blessed is the mother who gave you birth and nursed you!" She was a mother herself, likely, or perhaps she earnestly desired to be a mother. She imagined what it must have been like to be Jesus's mother. What blessing that must have been!

But Jesus would have none of it. His reply was brief and blunt. "Blessed rather are those who hear the word of God and obey it" (Luke 11:27–28). He immediately shifted the focus away from his mother and the quintessential acts of mothering—birth and breast-feeding, which are humbling acts of the most primal service—to something even more essential: spiritual relationship to himself. Far more important than serving as his mother, and even more important than motherhood itself, is hearing and obeying God's Word. This is something that all people, women and men, can aspire to.

TEACHING OUR CHILDREN TO SERVE

Ironically, in our desire to be Jesus to our family, we can undermine the very gift we hope to give our children. Behind much of our service is not only our desire to be like Christ, but also our hope that, in serving our children, they will learn to serve. But it is possible to give ourselves so fully to our families that they only learn to take what we give. They will determine that the world exists to meet their needs. And so we must teach them to serve, not just by serving them, but also by encouraging them to serve. This might involve our setting a better example of *receiving* from others even when we feel we should be giving.

I am writing this chapter now because of my husband's service to me. He stayed in town today instead of flying to a meeting so I would have time to write. He will pick up the kids from school, make dinner, and take them target shooting after dinner so I can finish my work. On Sunday mornings, when I am busy preparing to teach a class at church, Duncan is in the kitchen, concocting my morning latte. He sends a mug, steaming, with whipped cream and cinnamon on top, upstairs to my office in the hands of one of the kids, who delight in serving me. My children have learned from this. On Mother's Day, all of the kids shower me with gifts and handmade cards. One Valentine's Day when Duncan was gone, Naphtali, then eleven, secretly gathered all her money and walked alone three miles to the store and back in the near dark to bring me a bouquet of roses. I cried.

> Even in my weakness I am living out before my children the most essential truth of our lives: all of us are in severe need of this glorious and merciful Savior.

This is how we live out Christ to one another. Not by stealing Jesus's authority or assuming his omniscience but by humbly serving—children serving parents, parents serving children, husbands serving wives, wives serving husbands. And when my own servant's heart is emptied, as it often is when I stand among my family's continual needs, I am reminded that I cannot *be* Jesus; I can only *need* Jesus. In the times when I feel as though I fail most—when I dissolve before my children into anger and helplessness—he covers and forgives my exhaustion, sin, and limitations. He teaches me that his own work in my children's lives is not dependent upon me, that even in my weakness I am living out before my children the most essential truth of our lives: all of us are in severe need of this glorious and merciful Savior.

For Reflection and Discussion

1. Are you more likely to be tempted toward exercising unbiblical authority with your child or toward unhealthy servanthood? Describe a time when you gave in to that temptation. How did it affect your relationship with your child? Your feelings about your parenting abilities?

2. How does our culture, particularly within the Christian community, promote the idea that we should have complete authority and influence over our children? How does our culture promote the idea that we can "do it all" as we serve our family?

Read Jeremiah 17:7–10 and Philippians 2:5–8.

3. What do these verses suggest about how God calls you to relate to your child?

4. How do you discern the difference between maintaining a healthy parental authority and exercising an unbiblical power over your child?

Read Luke 10:38–42.

5. Describe a time you served someone else at the expense of your relationship with God.

6. How might your service to your family *teach* your child to serve others? How might your service to your family *prevent* your child from serving others?

7. Describe a time when you found it difficult to receive practical help from a friend or family member. How did you handle the situation? How might you handle similar situations in light of what you've learned in this chapter?

8. In what ways could you help your children understand that you rely on God for help in your parenting?

9. In what specific situation might you need to pull back from assuming unbiblical authority in your family right now? In what specific situation might you need to pull back from unhealthy servanthood in your family right now?

You Will Always Feel Unconditional Love for Your Children

How Our False Ideas of Love Burden Us with Guilt

Lisa, a single mother, is weary. More than six years ago her son, Kevin, entered the terrible twos, and he has remained there ever since, resisting her on everything from the way the eggs are fixed for breakfast to getting to school on time. He will not wear a coat even though it is forty-five degrees outside and raining. She has learned to let this go. She drives Kevin and his ten-year-old sister to school, trying hard to be bright, to send them off with cheer. Her daughter, Camille, joins her in singing along with the radio, but Kevin only grumbles. As the kids leave the car, Lisa calls out, "Have a terrific day!" Camille smiles back. Kevin turns his face away and marches to the playground. He will likely be sent to time-out at least once today, probably more. Lisa sighs as she watches his small body, suddenly animated, approach his friends. She knows her hours at work will pass quickly and the conflict will begin again as soon as he comes home.

Lisa is brought to secret tears by Kevin's oppositional will nearly every day. *I still love him,* she thinks as she waits for some tenderness to bubble up in her. But it does not come. In the next second, guilt kicks in. He's only eight years old. How can that deep baby-love already be gone? In a near whisper, Lisa dares to ask, "What kind of mother am I that I don't feel love for my son?" She is frightened.

> As soon as I march up to the boys and pull them apart, barking, a voice in my head says, *A perfect mother wouldn't do this.*

At my house, the three older boys are teasing each other again. Soon it will escalate until someone is crying...or worse. As soon as I march up to the boys and pull them apart, barking, a voice in my head says, *A perfect mother wouldn't do this.* Then, rather than scoff at the idea of a perfect mother (I should know better than to think there is such a thing), I think of one in my church. No, I think of two women I know. No, now it is three. Women who are calm and loving and patient without fail. Women I've never seen angry. I cannot imagine them saying what I am saying right now: "I told you to get to your rooms! Nobody's coming out for an hour. And if you miss dinner, too bad!" I try to imagine Joyce saying this, but I can't. Amy? No, she would never. I failed again in venting my anger, and my anger scares me. Even more, I don't feel love right now. Not now, not this whole week even, as the boys' antics and wrangling have shaken the house while Duncan is gone. I tell myself that if I truly loved my children, my feelings wouldn't wax and wane as they do.

Where is the unconditional love for my children that I expected? Even when my children were young and I was deep in a sugary baby-love, I experienced times of disappointment. My toddlers' defiance and endless questions often brought me to the end of my patience. Where is the love that God requires, the same unconditional love I have received from him, my own heavenly parent? Don't I know that of all the virtues, love comes first?

I can rehearse on command the biblical calls to love: "Love the Lord your God with all your heart and with all your soul and with all your strength and with all your mind" and "Love your neighbor as yourself" (Luke 10:27). "The fruit of the Spirit is love, joy, peace…" (Galatians 5:22–23). "Love covers over a multitude of sins" (1 Peter 4:8). "Live a life of love" (Ephesians 5:2). "God is love" (1 John 4:8). I also know that God's love is perfect and unchanging. God describes himself as "the Father of the heavenly lights, who does not change like shifting shadows" (James 1:17). God's love is so perfect that he cannot love me any more today than he did yesterday, my pastor preaches in a sermon. "God's love is so perfect, there is nothing I can do to alter his love for me," Christian radio assures.

I hang my head in condemnation. I do not love my children this way. The fault, clearly, must be mine. But I am discovering that these verses are not the whole truth about God's love. I return to Scripture, beginning in the Old Testament, where we read the testimony of God's great Father-love for Israel.

GOD'S COMPLICATED LOVE

Moses wrote poetically of God's tender love for Israel, his child:

> In a desert land he found him,
>   in a barren and howling waste.
> He shielded him and cared for him;
>   he guarded him as the apple of his eye,
> like an eagle that stirs up its nest
>   and hovers over its young,
> that spreads it wings to catch them
>   and carries them on its pinions.
>   (Deuteronomy 32:10–11)

Such a portrait of God's fatherly and motherly love! He was a doting parent, not removed from the dust of the earth by his transcendence and perfection. He showed a mother's tenderness as he cared for his firstborn—shielding, guarding, hovering over his young, catching and carrying them to safety when danger nears.

This is the kind of parent I want to be; this is the kind of love I want to live out. And we do live out this kind of love when our children are small and helpless, when we are their legs, their arms, their shield. But if we know the Old Testament at all, we know this tenderness was not returned in Israel's case. Just a few verses later, Moses wrote of this son's response to God's extraordinary paternal and maternal love:

> He [Israel] abandoned the God who made him
>   and rejected the Rock his Savior....
> You deserted the Rock, who fathered you;
>   you forgot the God who gave you birth.
>   (Deuteronomy 32:15, 18)

The Israelites' sin was unimaginably great: desertion, abandonment, rejection of the love of the One who had given them life, who had lavished a perfect and undeserved love upon them, who had saved them from slavery and brought them into a new land.

If we did not know the whole story of Israel's relationship with God, what might we imagine God's response to be? Schooled in our twenty-first-century, New Testament–only version of biblical love, we might think only of verses such as "Love is patient, love is kind.... It keeps no record of wrongs" (1 Corinthians 13:4–5). We would be certain of God's unwavering tenderness. But God did not wink his eye lovingly and forgetfully at Israel's disobedience. He responded unequivocally to their rejection:

> The LORD saw this and rejected them
>> because he was angered by his sons and daughters.
> "I will hide my face from them," he said,
>> "and see what their end will be;
> for they are a perverse generation;
>> children who are unfaithful....
> I will heap calamities upon them....
> I will send wasting famine against them."
>> (Deuteronomy 32:19–20, 23–24)

In Jeremiah 12:7–8 God offered further warnings of what he would do because of the Israelites' unfaithfulness:

> I will forsake my house,
>> abandon my inheritance;

I will give the one I love
    into the hands of her enemies.
My inheritance has become to me
    like a lion in the forest.
She roars at me;
    therefore I hate her.

Isaiah reports this:

In his love and mercy he redeemed them....
Yet they rebelled
    and grieved his Holy Spirit.
So he turned and became their enemy
    and he himself fought against them.
        (Isaiah 63:9–10)

The ground shifts beneath us. Not only was God fully expressive of passionate love for his children, but within that passionate love, he also expressed hate. Hate? How could a God described as the personification of love itself become an enemy to his own children? These are not rare verses. Elsewhere in Scripture, God's response to his called-out people includes disgust, sorrow, lament, and fury.

Yes, you may say, but that's all Old Testament, the old covenant, the age of law and justice. The New Testament began the age of grace, a fuller expression of God's love. Didn't Christ passively give himself over to the wicked, dying for all as the ultimate expression of God's unconditional love?

That's true, but we often view Jesus through the eyes of a contemporary culture that desires a Savior who is passive and nonjudgmental, who is simple rather than complex. We love the passages that reveal Christ's deep longing for his children. "O Jerusalem, Jerusalem, you who kill the prophets and stone those sent to you, how often I have longed to gather your children together, as a hen gathers her chicks under her wings, but you were not willing" (Matthew 23:37). In these words we hear the echo of God the Father's heart in the Old Testament when he said of Israel, "All day long I have held out my hands to an obstinate people" (Isaiah 65:2).

We forget, though, that this New Testament expression of love immediately follows seven ringing pronouncements of judgment upon that generation for their lack of faith. To the Pharisees who were creating their own template for righteousness, Jesus boldly proclaimed: "Woe to you, teachers of the law and Pharisees, you hypocrites! You are like whitewashed tombs... You snakes! You brood of vipers! How will you escape being condemned to hell?" (Matthew 23:27, 33). Jesus had strong words for all his disciples as well: "All men will hate you because of me" and "Anyone who does not take his cross and follow me is not worthy of me" (Matthew 10:22, 38).

To those hoping for a Savior who would bring peace and comfort and security, Jesus warned, "Do not suppose that I have come to bring peace to the earth. I did not come to bring peace, but a sword. For I have come to turn 'a man against his father, a daughter against her mother, a daughter-in-law against her mother-in-law—a man's enemies will be the members of his own household'" (Matthew 10:34–36).

These verses, and many others like them, reveal a theology that challenges our feel-good concept of biblical love. Despite the harshness of these portions of Scripture, they have much to teach us about loving our children. We must understand them, even if they stretch and challenge our most basic assumptions.

THREE NOTIONS ABOUT LOVE

Faced with Scriptures that proclaim "God is love" and Scriptures that include multiple examples of God's judgments and destructions, we may conclude that Scripture is contradictory. Or we may conclude that our concept of love is horribly wrong.

I believe we have made significant errors in our thoughts about God and his love. And I do not have to travel far to find these mistaken ideas; I have held them all myself. From our culture and even from our churches, many of us have absorbed notions about love that look nothing like true biblical love. And it has had profound effects upon our parenting.

Here are three ways we think of love—all containing some degree of truth—and the devastating conclusions we draw from them when they become distorted.

1. Love feels good.

Whether it's through a romantic comedy, a Hallmark family movie, or an MTV music video, our culture tells us that love feels good. Love brings you stuff: flowers, dinners out, expensive chocolate, fancy cars. Love is fun and takes you to the beach, the ski slopes, the races. Love fulfills all your emptiness and longings. Love completes you and bestows peace and joy.

> From our culture and even from our churches, many of us have absorbed notions about love that look nothing like true biblical love. And it has had profound effects upon our parenting.

But these portraits are far removed from our daily lives as parents. When we hold tight to a rule despite protests, when our children resent the boundaries we've erected for their protection, when we persevere beyond our own exhaustion to provide for them, we probably won't experience feelings of love or joy or peace. While we may know in our minds that these disciplines are acts of love, our negative feelings steal our certainty and hold us hostage. We conclude: *Love is supposed to feel good. Raising my child is difficult and I don't always feel good about her. Therefore, I must not love my child.*

2. Love is not a feeling.

Recognizing the fallout from our culture's obsession with love as a good feeling, the church has staked its tent on more solid ground. Emotions are not to be trusted. Weak and wavering, they are often the seat of our fallen nature. Instead, we understand that love is a decision. Love is commitment. Love is action. All of this is based on God's love, which is founded not on emotion but on choice. He chose us before the foundation of the world. We love him because he first loved us. He is the initiator; we are the receivers.

Even here, on this solid biblical footing, as parents we feel condemned: *How do I know my actions represent love if I can't rely on my feelings? How long must I continue making the choice to love without any motivating emotion behind it? What do I do with these intense emotions if they aren't supposed to represent love?*

3. Love is holy, perfect, and unchanging.

As we examine biblical love more closely, we discover that God's love lacks nothing. Scripture tells us that he is unchangeable: "I the LORD do not change" (Malachi 3:6). The psalmists declared over and over that "the LORD is good;

his love endures forever." The perfection of God's love gives us great comfort as his children. But as parents seeking to emulate God as he requires—"Be perfect, therefore, as your heavenly Father is perfect" (Matthew 5:48)—we fail continually. We realize: *I can't maintain a consistent calm in the face of my child's sinful behavior. I haven't landed on a consistent approach to discipline that seems effective. My feelings about my children are often wavering and conflicting. I have failed, then, in loving my children as consistently as God loves.*

No matter where we land among these ideas, we end up losing. So is it impossible to love our children unconditionally? No. While each of these concepts expresses some aspect of truth, these truths are incomplete. A closer look at Scripture leads us into fuller truth—truth that begins in the person of God himself.

WE HAVE OVERSIMPLIFIED LOVE

When we focus on God's sovereignty and omnipotence, as we should, we imagine God as dispassionate, holding to his preordained course through human history with nary a quiver of emotion. But emotions are God's idea and God's creation, not Satan's nor ours. Made in his image, we feel because he feels; our emotions are part of what we share with his own nature.

Even so, the New Testament proclamation that "God is

love" does not mean that God floats on an emotional high, reveling in his warm feelings for his children regardless of their behavior. God's love does not lift him beyond the sins and rebellion of his children. Just the opposite. God's love draws him near to his rebellious children.

Following our culture, and our own selective reading of God's Word, we have committed a grievous error: we have assigned an emotional simplicity to God that diminishes his majesty and tarnishes his glory. God's love is not a single emotion. God's love not only embraces a range of emotions and responses but in fact *requires* a range of emotions and responses. *Because* God the Father loved his children the Israelites, he was infuriated by their sin, which hurt and destroyed them as well as others. *Because* he loved his children and desired their highest good—that they would know him and find their delight in him—he angrily punished their idolatry. *Because* he loved his children, his heart was broken.

All of this filters down to our own families. Though we may not always feel a deep, unconditional love for our children, that does not mean we love them any less. When our children disobey, when they cause harm to another, when they choose attitudes and actions that cut against the holiness that God desires, we will have an emotional response—if we truly love them. Loving them means that we desire their highest good: to know God and live righteously before him. We may feel anger, as God does. We may feel hurt, as God does. We may feel disgust, as God does. Love not only allows these feelings; it requires them.

> We may feel anger, as God does. We may feel hurt, as God does. We may feel disgust, as God does. Love not only allows these feelings; it requires them.

None of this means that our anger and impatience toward our children is always justified. God's own expressions of anger and judgment do not instantly validate our own. At times our emotional responses to our children have as much to do with our failings and sin as theirs. Our frustrations must also be tempered by the recognition that children are under construction, works in progress, just like us. They will make many mistakes in their journey to adulthood—mistakes that must be covered by grace and forgiveness.

LIVING OUT THE COMPLEXITY OF BIBLICAL LOVE

How do we live out this more complex understanding of biblical love? Let me return to where we live—our homes.

Lisa's daily battles with her oppositional son Kevin continue, but she does not give up. She continues singing in the car, hugging Kevin when she can, and holding firm on household rules, despite his constant challenges. The absence of good feelings toward her son does not scare her as much. She remembers God's own persistent love to his iron-necked children Israel and is reminded that real biblical love perseveres. And that her feelings, however negative and changeable, are most of all a sign that she does indeed care about Kevin. She hopes that her love for him will be reciprocated someday. But even if that doesn't happen, she knows her hope in God will not be disappointed.

At my house two boys are teasing each other about girl-friends. The talk gets insulting, taunting, mostly from the elder to the younger. The younger son retreats, crushed and crying, but silently, knowing his tears will be another cause of jeers. I have heard most of the exchange. When I see my younger son hurt again, my heart is pierced. I am furious with the older son, who should be beyond this by now. I stride into his room, working at controlling my anger, determined to be fair but just. I speak with him; he defiantly defends himself. Attempting to be calm, I deliver the news: he is grounded for a week. He rolls his eyes and throws his books to the floor in protest as I leave.

As I return to work, my stomach is tight, my face is set. Have I blown it again? I feel guilty for the negative emotions that wash over me. I feel anything but warm and loving. But I know by now that I don't need to attack myself for these feelings or question my love for both sons. I know from Scripture and from God's own parenting that loving another doesn't always feel good. That it isn't always soft or pretty. That love wounds as much as it heals. My circumstances, my personality, the rivalries among my sons—none of this has changed. But I am freed from the internal accusations and feelings of disappointment that haunted me for so long. I do not think about the women in my church who appear to be perfect. I ask myself instead, *Will my discipline bring my son closer to being the person God wants him to be?* Toward that end, I know there must be consequences for his actions and words. Later, when his spirit is more open, I will try to talk with him again.

Why do we wonder at the depth and complexity of raising children? I am certain no other work on earth calls forth such deep, conflicting emotions. But even in these emotions we are in good company—in the company of a Father who has allowed us to hear his own breaking, loving heart as he continually extends himself to his children.

For Reflection and Discussion

1. What do current movies, television shows, and commercials suggest about how love is given and received?

2. Describe a recent time when you felt guilty for being angry with your child. Do you believe your feelings of guilt were justified? Why or why not?

Read Isaiah 63:9–10.

3. What emotions did God experience in his relationship with Israel, as described in these verses?

4. In what way(s) are these emotions similar to or different from how your current Christian community views God's love?

5. Why did God's love for Israel lead to anger?

6. How does the knowledge that God's love led him to feel not only anger but also grief over his child's behavior affect your view of your own parenting struggles?

7. How do you distinguish between healthy anger toward your child and unhealthy anger?

8. Consider a recurring struggle you have with your child. In what ways does loving your child require you to experience a range of emotions in that situation?

9. What are some actions you must take as a parent that may not feel loving yet are a necessary expression of your love for your child?

Successful Parents
Produce Godly Children

The Danger of Making Too Much of
Ourselves and Too Little of God

Duncan and Noah were at the cannery store. It's a thirty-minute boat trip we make about once a week in the summer for mail and supplies. Duncan had to get groceries from the cannery, and Noah, seven, had to get a present for his sister, who was turning nine. He had a little money in his pocket, money he'd earned from working in the fishing boat with us. There's not a lot for kids at Larsen Bay Mercantile, a small store mostly for fisherman, located in a creaky one-hundred-year-old wooden building set on pilings. One corner, though, has a few toys and coloring books. Noah knew this section well. He found something his sister would like—a set of colored erasers—and asked Duncan how much it was.

"It's three dollars, Noah," Duncan said after peering at the price tag. "Do you have three dollars?"

"Nope. I've only got two." Noah stood for a moment fingering his money. Then suddenly he stuffed the money back into his pocket and began wiggling a loose tooth, his mouth cranked open, his eyes focused in concentration. In less than a minute he held the tooth in hand, bloody at one end, and extended it without a word to Duncan. An astonished Duncan (our family tooth fairy) took the tooth, fished out the last needed dollar from his own pocket, and the purchase was made.

When Duncan returned from the store with Noah's tooth in his pocket and this story, I laughed. Another example of Noah's determination and perseverance, traits we had worked hard to encourage. My mother's heart thumped gratefully in rhythm with the invisible pats I delivered to my own back. *See what we've taught him? We must be doing something right!* But then I frowned. *Wait! He's selling body parts, and his father's buying them. Isn't that just a little too stoic and intense for a seven-year-old? What have we done? Maybe we're working him too hard. Maybe we've overdone the "finish whatever you start" shtick. Maybe we're trying to grow him up too fast...*

THE INNER COURTROOM

Even in the most innocuous of events with my children, I erect an internal courtroom almost instantly, complete with lawyers, a jury, and a judge. I haven't yet reached a verdict in this instance, but I have on many other happy occasions— and plenty of unhappy occasions when my children's behavior has been less than inspiring. At those times the verdict is clear and instantaneous: my children's behavior is the product of bad parenting. Guilty! The gavel falls. But if the verdict is good, I prance off guilt-free, proud of my extraordinary children and my oh-so-brilliant parenting.

Why do so many of us do this? Why are we poised over every event, ready to prophesy the future, ready to render judgment on our children's performance—and on our own performance as a parent? It's hardly surprising, given the magnitude of our endeavors. What other enterprise binds children and adults in a twisting helix of shared DNA, bathrooms, car keys, dreams, meals, vacations, and crises? Children possess our hearts, feed our hearts, twist our hearts into a thousands shapes, and we let it all happen. We have to— they are our children. But how do we know if we are doing a good job? How can we measure the success of this lifelong labor?

Parents as Winner and Losers

One common reaction to the question that haunts so many of us is to examine the fruit of our efforts. "If our parents' approach *seemed* close to biblical parenting, yet bore bad fruit, we can be certain it was not biblical," says one writer. We can know this, he asserts, because God's Word gives us exactly what we need to raise godly children. "Parents who accurately implement them [biblical principles] will not be disappointed."[1]

Another parenting writer advises us in an online Bible study to "observe and learn from winning parents." "Winning parents" are those whose children are "obedient" and "respectful," who "know God's will," who are Christians and "live faithful Christian lives." We should be imitating those parents "who are successful, not those who fail."[2]

Isn't this just as we thought and feared? Some parents are winners and some are losers. Which are you? Which am I? Many friends immediately come to mind. I think of three couples, all of whom love the Lord and all of whom have sons who have spent time in jail. They feel like failures as parents, though they all worked at raising their children in the admonition of the Lord. I think of Marla, working in Christian ministry, who was widowed early in her marriage. She continued in the ministry while raising her daughter alone. Her daughter rejected Christ early in her high school years and has held resolutely to her agnosticism ever since. Marla cannot account for her daughter's spiritual rebellion without blaming herself. She is consumed with guilt.

What happens when we take this spiritual outcomes assessment to its logical conclusion? As one author writes, our job as parents is "to raise spiritual champions."[3] There is much at stake, says the writer. "In your mind, have you accepted the responsibility for changing a small part of the world through your children?"[4] To maximize our ability to produce spiritual champions, the author creates a model based on surveys, statistical studies, and personal interviews. His research reveals that a small family is better than a large family, the firstborn is the most likely to become a spiritual giant, and single-parent homes are seldom successful in producing faith champions.[5] The book ends with these motivational words: "Between you and your spouse, have you covered the ground necessary to produce children whose lives honor God and advance his kingdom?"[6]

> When will I know if I am producing children whose lives will honor God and advance his kingdom?

I confess to feeling flummoxed by these admonitions. When will I know if I am producing children whose lives will honor God and advance his kingdom? What is the "necessary ground" that must be covered to be successful—and once I cover it, is the rest truly guaranteed?

God's Spiritual Heroes

Again, we must turn to God's Word. What do the Scriptures say about "spiritual champions"?

Hebrews 11, the great Hall of Faith chapter, provides just such a list, where the author identifies men and women who through extraordinary faith, "conquered kingdoms, administered justice...shut the mouths of lions, quenched the fury of the flames...whose weakness was turned to strength.... Others were tortured and refused to be released.... They were stoned; they were sawed in two.... They went about...destitute, persecuted and mistreated." In short, "The world was not worthy of them" (Hebrews 11:32–38).

The immensity of their faith is so stunning: surely these individuals were raised by wise, God-fearing, faith-filled parents. Surely they were the same kind of parent to their own children. Yet as I consider the lives of these heroes, I am not sure I can reach that conclusion.

- Abraham was impatient for the son God promised. Urged on by his wife, he sired a child by her maidservant, Hagar, and allowed this woman and his own son Ishmael to be banished to the desert.

- Isaac and Rebekah were the parents of Jacob and Esau. Each openly favored one son over the other. Rebekah, lacking faith in God's ability to overcome

Isaac's favoritism, instructed Jacob to commit an unthinkable travesty: to lie to his father and steal the blessing from Esau, which he did.

- Jacob learned his lessons well from his mother and continued to deceive his way toward success—lying to Esau, lying to Laban, and treating his wives and his ten sons with inequity.

- Moses was pulled from his basket on the Nile by the daughter of the pharaoh. God chose for him to be raised by a woman who worshiped many gods and who taught Moses to do the same.

- Jephthah, a mighty warrior for God, was born to a prostitute. As a father, he killed his only daughter as a sacrifice to God because of an impetuous vow.

Many more examples in the Scriptures confound our parenting expectations, but two must be mentioned:

- Jonathan, David's closest friend, was the son of King Saul, a man who turned from God and descended into solipsistic and murderous rebellion. Jonathan's righteousness and purity could not have contrasted more starkly with his father's dark sin.

- Josiah, the boy king, was the son of Amon, a man who "did evil in the eyes of the LORD" (2 Kings 21:20). Yet Josiah, of all the kings of Judah, was the most righteous, a king who was singularly commended as one who served the Lord "with all his heart and with all his soul and with all his strength" (2 Kings 23:25).

By our contemporary standards, most of these families were dismal failures. They include polygamous family groupings rife with division and jealousy, prostitute mothers, heathen mothers, families with rampant favoritism and fratricide. The only discernible patterns here seem to be those of human sin and error. Yet God transformed their weaknesses into a faith that accomplished his eternal purposes.

> God will use every aspect of my human parenting, even my sins and failures, to shape my children into who he desires them to be, for the sake of his kingdom.

Here is what I learn from this: I am not sovereign over my children—God is. And God will use every aspect of my human parenting, even my sins and failures, to shape my children into who he desires them to be, for the sake of his kingdom.

Does God Pass Our Parenting Test?

As I wrote earlier, this book grew out of my inner wrestlings on the day when I stood in a spruce forest crying out my disappointment and frustration to God. Disappointment that I wasn't a better mother and that my children weren't better children. Frustration that no one in my house measured up to what our Christian communities seemed to expect.

Then came a sudden recognition that much of the load I was carrying wasn't meant to be carried and that some of that load may not have come from Scripture, as I had believed. Four years after that initial thought, this understanding still appears valid.

The Old Testament provides a long and deep look into the heart of the only perfect parent—God himself. In the Bible, God identifies himself over and over as a Father. When we look at his children, however, the news is not good. Beginning with Adam and Eve and moving through history, the story doesn't improve. By the days of Noah, God's people had so polluted the world with their wickedness that God regretted having made them. He ended the lives of every man, woman, and child who was not faithful to him. God birthed another family later, the children of Israel, whom God called "my firstborn son" (Exodus 4:22). We know the tortuous record of that relationship, involving children who rebelled against their Father grievously.

Our own record as God's children is not much better. What shall we say for ourselves? Shall we point to our own pure hearts whose sole desire is to serve God with all of our being? No. If God's success as a parent is to be judged by us, his children, what can we conclude? God himself does not pass our parenting test.

TOO MUCH OF OURSELVES AND TOO LITTLE OF GOD

We know, then, that there is serious error in our assumptions. We have made far too much of ourselves and far too little of God. We have adopted our culture's belief that we are the primary shapers of our children and that we have control over who they are and who they will become.

John Rosemond, a family psychologist and syndicated columnist, hears frequently from parents who believe they have failed when their children have problems. "They think this," he writes, "because they believe in psychological determinism—specifically, that parenting produces the child. This is absurd. Parenting is an influence. It is not the be-all, end-all influence."[7]

Many of us as Christian parents have drifted into "spiritual determinism": we have followed our culture's belief in psychological determinism but spiritualized it with Bible verses. This reflects our sinful bent to see ourselves as more essential and more in control than we actually are. It's also our heritage as Americans, Harriet Lerner observes in her book *The Mother Dance*. As good Americans, we believe that we can fix every problem, that we are the masters over our own fate. The root of much of our pain in parenting is "the belief that we should have control over our children, when it is hard enough to have control over ourselves."[8]

This reflex to judge ourselves by our children, and to judge others by their children, has further implications: it reveals a faulty view of spiritual formation. We often expect that children of believing parents will show the same kind of attitudes and behavior we expect to see in each other: love, joy, peace, patience, perseverance, kindness, and obedience, as a beginning list. One writer suggests that parents have just thirteen years to win or lose the spiritual battle in their child's heart.[9]

How is it we expect children of Christians to consistently demonstrate spiritual maturity? Even when a child makes his own decision to follow Christ, we often expect visible and even immediate transformation. The Bible demonstrates another reality.

WHAT DO WE EXPECT?

Even after four decades of desert wanderings, the Israelites continued to rebel against God. In the New Testament the disciples lived in the presence of Jesus for three years. How many miracles did they witness, how many resurrections, how many teachings before they understood that he was who he said he was?

Why do we expect our children to be finished products when they proclaim any level of belief in Christ? Why do we expect even children who have not yet professed faith in Christ to live and act like mature believers? Like us, our children were born in sin and they are dead in their sins until they turn to God and repent. Spiritual transformation is never accomplished by the wave of a wand but through persistence and the working of God's Spirit in a willing spirit over time. When Jesus uttered "It is finished" from the cross, redemption was fully accomplished, but we are not finished in this life. Ever. Our transformation into the image of Christ goes on as long as we have breath—until we are in another body and finally "see him as he is" (1 John 3:2).

Knowing this brings great calm and freedom. It releases me from the frantic pressure I have felt to make sure my children "ask Jesus into their hearts." It releases me from the burden of believing that I am the primary shaper and molder of my children's hearts. It releases me from the panic that I've been given a deadline to produce spiritually complete human beings.

As our children enter adolescence, these truths about spiritual formation are especially needed. I have three teenagers at the moment. They are often wonderfully cooperative and mature, as many observers have remarked. There are times, though, when our family ship tips as my sons question our beliefs, rules, and lifestyle. Their questions are fair. Their experiments with hair, clothes, music, and other markers of identity are not threats but an essential part of their movement toward autonomy.

As believers, we often forget that our children enter a church and a faith practice through *our* choice and *our* faith, not their own. As they grow toward adulthood and independence, it is not only natural but necessary for them to examine the beliefs we claim. We need to extend grace to them as they begin a spiritual journey that might look different from our own. As they discover their own identities and find their place in the family and the world, our challenge is to look beyond the externals to their growing hearts and spirits—as God himself does.

When we engage in spiritual determinism and a human view of spiritual formation, we can easily fall into judging others. Jeanine, a friend I have known for years, has a sixth-grade daughter, Julia, a middle child in a large family. Her social skills are not well developed, Jeanine tells me, and she has few friends. Julia wanted to be friends with Krista, a girl from her church who lived fairly close to their home. They had gotten along well together on a number of occasions, but Krista declined Julia's every invitation to come over. Julia found out why one day when Krista's brother told her, "Krista will never go to your house. Our mother says you're demon-possessed!" Jeanine looked at me sadly. "Julia is just a normal girl who's struggling with her identity right now and who's looking for a friend. Some people—even in church—have already written her off. And she's only eleven years old." Jeanine felt the sting of judgment, knowing some in the church questioned her spirituality and her parenting because of her daughter's behavior.

I, too, am saddened by Jeanine's words. I have experienced this kind of judgment myself, as have many others whose children are moving through the usual and necessary stages of development and growth. We needn't try to take the Holy Spirit's place. Our job is not to judge and convict, but to love and encourage children—and their parents—all along the way, wherever they are in their faith journey.

WHETHER THEY LISTEN OR NOT

The question we ask of ourselves must be reframed. We need to quit asking, Am I parenting *successfully*? Instead we need to ask, Am I parenting *faithfully*? Faithfulness, after all, is what God requires most from us.

> We need to quit asking, Am I parenting *successfully*? Instead we need to ask, Am I parenting *faithfully*?

We see this clearly in the calling of Ezekiel. Though Ezekiel was not a parent (as far as we know), his calling to the people of Israel has remarkable parallels to our calling as parents.

Ezekiel's story begins on the banks of the Kebar River, where he was living in exile with other Israelites. God suddenly spoke to Ezekiel and revealed phantasmagoric visions of heaven. In these visions God himself appeared and commissioned Ezekiel as a prophet to his people. God warned the prophet that he was sending him to his own people, a "rebellious nation...; they and their fathers have been in revolt against me to this very day." Ezekiel's job was to communicate God's message of judgment to them, to say, "This is what the Sovereign LORD says" (see Ezekiel 2:3–4).

At this point, all seemed well and good. Ezekiel did not have to go to a foreign nation—he did not have to attend language school for two years! He didn't have to eat strange foods, things like grubs and frog's feet. God's only initial dietary requirement was that Ezekiel eat a scroll enscribed with prophetic words, which tasted "sweet as honey" in his mouth (see 3:3). All of this is just as we would expect: God calls us and therefore he makes the calling possible. Surely Ezekiel was assured of a good outcome. After all, he was directly called by God to this work.

But bad news followed. The scroll turned bitter in Ezekiel's stomach. God told him that the people of Israel, his own people, would not listen to him. "The house of Israel is not willing to listen to you because they are not willing to listen to me, for the whole house of Israel is hardened and obstinate" (3:7).

God was sending him to speak what no one might listen to! The job would be hard, then—harder than the prophet could have realized at first. But God didn't leave Ezekiel defenseless. He did not make the task easier; he made Ezekiel stronger. "I will make you as unyielding and hardened as they are. I will make your forehead like the hardest stone, harder than flint" (3:8–9).

Ezekiel's response to this was so human, so like my own. With the Spirit of the Lord upon him, he returned to his people on the banks of the river with "bitterness and in the anger of my spirit." And he "sat among them for seven days—overwhelmed" (3:14–15).

Ezekiel, a prophet of God—a righteous man!—was overwhelmed by what God had called him to. Even angry and bitter. These are words of hope for me, for any of us who are overwhelmed as parents, who at times experience the same feelings toward our own calling. It is not a sin to be overwhelmed; it is simply recognition of the responsibility God has given us.

What kind of outcome was possible for Ezekiel here? God had already said the people wouldn't listen. The destruction Ezekiel was to foretell over a period of several years would not be averted by his prophet's voice, however obedient he was. And every horrific prophecy did indeed come true. So how successful was he as a prophet? Ezekiel's mission looks like an utter failure. But God spoke ten words in this narrative that changed everything. As God commissioned Ezekiel to speak his words to Israel, three times he prefaced his commands with this phrase: "whether they listen or fail to listen" (2:5, 7; 3:11). One of those three times God completed the sentence: "Whether they listen or fail to listen—for they are a rebellious house—*they will know that a prophet has been among them*" (Ezekiel 2:5).

This was Ezekiel's responsibility before God: to live and speak and enact God's own words before the people in such a way that they might know he was a righteous man, a prophet of God. Through him, they would see and hear God's word. Ezekiel wanted more than this, of course. He desperately wanted to change their hearts, to turn them back to the living God and avert the appalling judgment and death that were coming. He must have prayed throughout his long prophetic vigils that *someone* would repent. The record does not tell us whether this happened, but Ezekiel was never accountable for the repentance of others. He was accountable only for his obedience.

HOW CAN WE KNOW IF WE ARE PARENTING SUCCESSFULLY?

We know by now that we are asking the wrong questions. We are so focused on ourselves—our own need for success and the success of our children—that we have come to view parenting as a performance or a test. We cannot pass the test, I'm afraid. If we're graded on a curve, we will always find parents and children who are more obedient, more joyful, and more peaceful. If we are graded on an absolute scale, then we all fail. This is why Jesus came. This is why we need a Savior. "By grace you have been saved, through faith—and this not from yourselves, it is the gift of God—not by works, so that no one can boast" (Ephesians 2:8–9). If even our ability to believe in God is given to us by God, then how much of parenting can we accomplish on our own? None.

We must rethink our calling. We are not capable of producing perfect followers of Christ, as if we were perfect ourselves. Our work cannot purchase anyone else's salvation or sanctification. Parents with unbelieving children, friends with children in jail, and the faith heroes in Hebrews 11 are all powerful reminders of this truth: our children will make their choices, God will be sovereign, and God will advance his kingdom.

It is my earnest hope that these truths will move our parenting out of the courtroom that is always in session in our hearts. I have wasted so much time and emotion quaking before that inner judge and jury! Through God's Word, I am freed to return to my first calling: to live out and speak the truths of God's words wherever I am, especially before my children, regardless of their response. Now I can focus more on my obedience than on my children's weaknesses. I am not as likely to give up when a child persists in willfulness. And I can continue trusting and relying upon God.

Who can I trust more than God? Before him, I can release my powerless clutch on my children and myself and return what has belonged to him all along. I can rest—we can *all* rest—secure in his hands. These are the hands of the One who has fearfully and wonderfully made every one of us. The hands of a judge who is perfect in justice and mercy. The hands of a Father who longs to lead his daughters and sons safely home to his side.

For Reflection and Discussion

1. What standards do you use to measure your performance as a parent? What standards do you use to assess your child's performance?

2. Do you believe that you are the primary influence on your child's spiritual life? Why or why not?

Read Hebrews 11:4–40.

3. What do each of the individuals in this passage have in common?

4. How would the people listed in Hebrews 11 measure up to the standards you set for yourself as a parent and as a Christian?

5. How have you seen God use your weaknesses to fulfill his purpose in your child?

Read Ezekiel 2:3–8.

6. What do God's words suggest about whether Ezekiel would be successful as a prophet?

7. In what ways is a parent like a prophet?

8. In what ways can your parenting change the world? In what ways is your parenting limited in its potential effect?

9. How would your daily interactions with your child change if you felt free to love him regardless of whether or not he responded to that love?

10. How might your relationship with your child change if your definition of parenting success valued personal faithfulness over visible results?

God Approves of Only One
Family Design

Why God Is Not Limited
by Imperfect Families

When I think of my childhood, I think of houses. My family moved a lot when I was growing up, from one old colonial house in New Hampshire to another. My father could not keep a job and had little interest in or concern for me or my five siblings, so my mother reluctantly became the breadwinner and decision maker.

When I was five years old, my mother began restoring the 200-year-old house we lived in at the time. A few years later, she was able to sell it at a profit. From then on, she worked arduously, teaching herself how to plumb, wire, build furniture and hearths, and replace roofs and foundations—whatever was needed for restoration and resale. My father would help when he was around, but the six of us kids served as her primary labor force. While our friends were playing, we were sanding floors, hanging and taping Sheetrock, tearing down walls, digging out old outhouses, and steaming and scraping layers of wallpaper off 150-year-old plaster.

Some of the houses we lived in lacked insulation; one didn't have running water. The house we lived in during my high school years had neither insulation nor heat except for one wood stove in the kitchen, leaving the other rooms below freezing through the long New Hampshire winters.

My five siblings and I did not know much about God during those years. We had little time for church—we were busy working on the houses and trying to survive as a family. Our father, who was first a Christian Scientist and later an atheist, left us many times over the years. We had few toys, fewer clothes, and not much food. Because we could not afford shampoo, we washed our hair with soap and were teased often about our stringy, greasy hair. We did have times of happiness—the camping trips my mother took us on every summer, the days we spent in the woods, the sledding and skating in winter—but our lives were far from perfect.

MEASURING UP

I know I am not alone in having a less-than-ideal childhood. Many of us are children of divorced parents (either literally or emotionally) or have emotional or physical abuse in our back-grounds. Others had an adolescence filled with wrong choices or perhaps such difficult financial circumstances that the memories of feeling out of place and needy are never far away.

Whatever our childhoods, our own families today may not measure up to the image we hold as a model. Our homes might include a child born outside of marriage, a blended family, a teenager in trouble with the law, or an alcoholic spouse. Even parents whose own parents live far away can feel as if they've fallen short of the ideal family design, especially when they hear the casual way friends talk about their extended family's involvement with their kids. Others have only one child and field many questions about whether that child is "spoiled." Some parents with many children hear remarks about how large their family is, as if there is one size that is just right. Any one of these situations can make a parent feel judged—on bad days, even like a failure.

My own family is unique in a number of ways. Duncan and I married while still in college. We started our married life working together in commercial fishing every summer, side by side in the boat. We delayed starting a family for ten years—much longer than any of our friends. Our childbearing stage of life took us, unexpectedly, into our midforties— far beyond our peers. When I pick up Micah, my youngest, at preschool, I'm twenty years older than most of the other parents. Because of the number of our kids, many people assume we homeschool, but we don't. We don't seem to fit any particular family model. Duncan and I both work in professions, but we work out of adjacent offices in our house. We transition from our professional lives in the winter to commercial salmon fishing in the Alaskan bush in the summer. Our children work with us in our family business. When most kids are playing Little League and going to camp, ours are piloting boats, pulling fish from the stormy sea, and working exhausting hours to help support our family.

Some of our family characteristics are unexpectedly God-given; some are by choice or need. None of them are wrong, but they are different from the current cultural model of the ideal family. The distinctions have caused me great discomfort at times, especially when it comes to the number of children in our home. After all, one of the markers of the ideal family is size. Currently the average American family has 2.034 children. Anyone with more than two children knows what happens when you cross that line.

During my last two pregnancies, I received numerous disparaging comments about the size of our family. At fish camp one neighbor, whom I hadn't seen for a while, asked me, "So, how many kids you got now?"

"Six," I replied bravely, knowing he wouldn't approve.

"Oh, that's too many!" he exclaimed in all seriousness.

I've also found that people with traditional work hours, gender roles, and schedules cannot understand the rhythm of our lives, including our travel and the flexibility Duncan and I have to step into each other's roles when one of us is away.

I have plenty of my own insecurities with our family structure and dynamic. I sometimes wish my children could have a summer like other kids. I worry that their childhood on an Alaskan island will limit their ability to succeed in the larger culture. Because of our family size, our resources are stretched. Duncan and I worry that we'll run out of energy with our last two boys as we parent intensively into our sixties. When I hear reports on the necessity of spending quality time with each child individually, I fret that I won't meet that requirement. I'm jealous, sometimes, of the time parents can spend with each child in a smaller family. Some days I question everything. Did we marry too young? Did we wait too long to have kids? The myth of the perfect home is never far from my mind, making every feature of our family a potential source of anxiety.

WHEN WE FEEL LIKE FAILURES

As I look at families around me, I see an amazing divergence from the "ideal." I know that many of us worry about our present differences and obsess over past mistakes and circumstances. William, a single father in New Hampshire with full custody of his daughter, confesses to an unending mental replay of his divorce and the resulting self-condemnation. He is working hard to raise his daughter well, but he feels like a failure already.

When another friend, Deborah, became pregnant with her boyfriend's baby, her dreams were shattered. She hoped to establish a Christian home with him—they were both believers—but he abandoned her and their child. She was sure that, as a single mother, her chance to achieve a Christian home and family was over.

Shelley adopted several children, with her husband's full support and urging, but the burden of the kids' needs overcame him. He emotionally—and sometimes physically—abandoned his family. Shelley feels guilty, overwhelmed, and responsible.

Added to the weight of current circumstances is the burden many of us carry from our own childhoods. Shelley, for instance, came from a broken home herself, raised by one parent in a divisive family. She was careful about who she married; she waited until the right man, a committed Christian, came along. Her sense of failure at her husband's distance is crushing. As for me, by the time I got into high school, my family seldom ate together. Now I'm obsessive about family dinners, scheduling them at any hour just so we can all sit down together. When my attempts fail and someone is still at practice or school, I worry that my children will scatter and divide as teenagers, as my siblings did.

If we end here, in inadequacy and fear, we can be paralyzed as parents. If we are vested in the biblical and cultural ideals of the family, and neither appears within reach, we can be tempted to give up. But surprising news from the Bible offers hope for all of us.

FAMILY VALUES?

Only one perfect family existed in history—and not for long. Adam and Eve knew God so intimately that they walked and conversed together in the garden in the cool of the evenings. But they rebelled, desiring to rule over their own lives rather than submit to God's rule. The effects were immediate. All of creation was ruptured. Husband and wife were divided from one another and driven from God's presence. The first child born into this fallen world killed his brother. The human family was forever changed.

> Only one perfect family existed in history—and not for long.

My American self, steeped in the current parenting literature, cannot make sense of this. Adam and Eve knew God intimately. Surely they taught their children about God! They alone could tuck their sons in at night with stories of strolling with God in the arbor, talking with him, working under his loving direction. Even after their sin, they were still living under God's family design: one man, one woman joined in marriage before God, raising their children to know and worship God. But none of this protected them, or their murdered son, from a brutal crime.

The biblical record of families does not improve from there. Genesis and Exodus alone take us through a dizzying assortment of family relationships and structures that include polygamy, concubinage, single parenting, divorce, sex with servants, gender segregation, and discrimination.

In fact, it's ironic that we often call our secular culture back to biblical family values when most families in the Bible looked nothing like our ideal of a family. Part of this discrepancy comes from the fact that issues of parenting and family are more complex and more culture-bound than we recognize.

How Families Used to Look

In the days of the Old Testament, families were defined far more broadly than our narrow nuclear family today. In Hebrew, the word for *family* is better translated "household," consisting of the patriarchal head, his wife or wives, servants, slaves, any children from those liaisons, and possibly other extended relatives. The households were multigenerational and communal, often sharing the same tents or dwellings, with none of the privacy that we assume is our right. Men and women ate separately, worshiped separately. Children did not inhabit the privileged and protected space they enjoy today.

They were regarded primarily as the property of the father. From an early age, they worked, spending most of their hours laboring in the fields, managing flocks of animals, helping in the unending tasks of surviving in an agrarian economy, even fighting in war. Children remained with their parents well into middle age, under their father's authority until the father died. The law of primogeniture awarded the father's assets and authority to the firstborn, leaving the other children mostly empty-handed. Women had no legal rights or property rights. Child labor, inequality, discrimination, and slavery were all common features of the Israelite culture.

From our twenty-first-century perspective, many of these realities, and the stories behind them, look like failure. How did God's people fail so decisively in their family lives? How did they create so many fractured variations of God's family design? Let's look at a prime example of a family that fell short—and what God did with it.

A Family Redeemed

Joseph, the wearer of the famous coat of many colors, was born into what today would be called a highly dysfunctional family. The son of Jacob and Rachel, he was the eleventh of twelve children. In this tumultuous household, he had only one full-blooded brother: Benjamin. The other ten were half brothers, sons of Jacob's first wife and two servants. The sons were shepherds from an early age, their work essential to the family's subsistence and survival, though it appears that Joseph and Benjamin were exempted from some of that labor.

Most of us know the story of Joseph and the coat his doting father bestowed on him—a visible testament of Jacob's undisguised favoritism. The brothers came to despise Joseph. We don't entirely blame them. Was he wearing the coat when he announced his triumphal dreams to his family, where sheaves of wheat, and the sun and stars, bowed down before him? Even Jacob could not stomach this vision or Joseph's tone as the young man breathlessly described his elders' future obeisance. The brothers may have suspected that Jacob would bequeath his goods, his blessing, and his authority to the eleventh son rather than to the eldest. For the elders to serve the younger would have been bitter indeed, overturning one of the central values of their culture.

It is not surprising, then, that the brothers plotted Joseph's death. He was thrown into a pit, and only through Reuben's pleadings was he sold into slavery instead of being killed. Joseph's path through Genesis wound through slavery, prison, and unimaginable suffering, until God dramatically lifted him from prison to the leadership of Egypt, second only to Pharaoh. Under Joseph's direction, all of Egypt, as well as his own family, survived a famine that could have devastated the entire region (Genesis 37; 41:53–42:3).

Joseph's extraordinary life ended in triumph as he embraced his brothers and returned love for hate, reconciliation for betrayal (Genesis 45). That clear light of redemption shines at the close of Joseph's account because his story began in such confusion and darkness. Joseph's family included polygamy, concubinage, jealousy, favoritism, deception, and attempted fratricide. In later years, the brothers would add further dysfunction and sin to this family record. Yet these same men became the founders of the new nation of Israel. It is Joseph whom we hold up as a beautiful example of God's will accomplished. And so we must amend our assumption that pain and sin in a family limit what God can do—with the truth of what he *has* done in such families, time and time again.

> We must amend our assumption that pain and sin in a family limit what God can do—with the truth of what he *has* done in such families, time and time again.

Where Do Our Standards Come From?

The biblical record is clear: our fallenness is all-pervasive. All believers through all generations have struggled to form biblical families within their own cultural context. Circumstances, culture, our own sins, and the sins of others affect what our homes look like. Yet we continue to put pressure on ourselves to make our families fit an elusive mold. We continue to believe, somewhere deep in our souls, that God is disappointed with our family if it does not fit the perfect Christian structure.

Well-meaning people in the church can contribute to our feelings of inadequacy. Some Christian organizations, for instance, teach that women please God primarily through marriage and motherhood. Growing numbers of organizations and couples oppose contraception, prescribing families as large as God can build. (I have personally been chastised for trying to limit my family through birth control.) The standards for the ideal Christian family often extend further to admonitions regarding gender roles, employment, and education. I know at least one group that discourages women of any age, even single women, from entering the work force lest they attempt to "serve two masters": their father or husband and their employer.[1]

But what damage do we cause when we suggest that God prescribes just one family model? My friend Sherie tried to hold her marriage together for fourteen years before her husband's abuse finally made it impossible. She tells me that her church pulled away from her during the difficult divorce proceedings, not wanting to condone the breakup of her marriage. Chad is fearful of revealing his wife's mental illness to his church, though he and their four children are in great need of assistance. Kevin and Amber love their family life, with Amber working full time outside the home while Kevin stays home with their two preschoolers. But they have trouble finding a place in their church because so many families function differently than theirs. Jane, a single mother, tells me she often feels that others regard her with suspicion. Another friend who chose to have only one child tells me that women in her church have never accepted her as a mother.

I don't believe we hurt people intentionally. Behind our concern for the family is our concern for the health of our country and for the next generation. We want to give all children the most secure environment, the most loving attention, the best chance to grow up as people who love God and serve him with their whole hearts. Never would we want to diminish this God-given ache of our hearts! We also know that many people would like to alter the traditional family as we know it. In the midst of these attacks, we rise up to protect family life. We celebrate families with a husband and wife who love each other and their children. But we must not privilege a narrowly defined model of the Christian family, punishing all others. Our less-than-ideal or simply unusual families can serve God's great purposes. We must not worship one family model. We are called to worship God alone.

GOD IS BIGGER THAN OUR WEAKNESSES

Within the kingdom of God, a variety of God-honoring family structures are not only possible but in fact beneficial to both the church and the needy world. Whether those unique families develop because of sinful choices or godly choices, God works through them.

This should not surprise us. Not only does God's Word offer countless examples of men and women of faith from many kinds of families, but indeed the principle of unity within diversity is central to the New Testament's teachings. The church itself is often represented as a physical body that is made of "many parts, but one body" (1 Corinthians 12:20).

I have learned so much from the Lord through my husband and six children, but I recognize that those in other family structures learn much from God as well. I know a couple on the mission field who raised only one child so they could spend more time ministering to others. Other families live in Christian communities, choosing to relinquish their own autonomy for the larger good of the church. Many families in my town live in multigenerational and extended family units, stressing interdependence rather than individualism. Other friends choose to adopt, bringing children from impoverished backgrounds into the warmth of their own home. These families understand more fully than I do about our adoption into God's family.

We must shed the myth that only a "perfect" family structure will guarantee the outcome of godly children, silence the attackers of the traditional family, and strengthen our national fabric. When we recognize the beautiful, redeemed variety of families in God's kingdom, we are free to embrace what God is doing in our own homes. Our limitations do not limit God.

WHAT GOD CAN DO

My own family of origin has taught me this truth. Into the hardship of my family life, God came. When I was thirteen, I heard the gospel at a sledding party. The moment I heard it, I knew it was true. The veil over life—obscuring something real I could not see but I knew was there—was finally rent. God became real. I grabbed hold of his presence and promises and have not looked back.

Our family life continued to be far from any kind of model. Yet it was hardship that schooled my heart to seek after what was true and lasting. Four of us gave our lives to the Lord while I was at home. Today, out of this broken family of eight, seven of us know God is our salvation and live to serve him.

Let me tell you of others. Devie grew up near me in New Hampshire. Her parents were both on their third marriage. The mother was a lapsed Catholic; her father claimed no particular faith. They divorced when Devie was eight and began shuttling Devie back and forth between homes. Her father had a conversion experience not long after the divorce. He began taking his daughter to church. She, too, put her faith in Christ. The father did not remain in his faith, however, and several years later moved on to another marriage, dropping his church activities and Christian friends. Devie did not. She continued going to church, unwavering in her faith. She finished high school and went on to graduate from a Christian college, ready to serve God wherever he took her.

Jim's childhood was a nightmare. His alcoholic father came home one day and tried to kill his mother with a hammer. When he was five, his parents divorced. His mother then married an obsessively controlling man who cared little for her kids. When Jim was nine, his mother died and his stepfather abandoned Jim and his siblings, leaving them penniless and alone. The rest of his growing-up years he lived with foster families, where he never felt loved or cared for. Though Jim was not yet a Christian, he felt the presence of God with him throughout his suffering. It was the absence of a loving family that brought him to the Lord, he says in his autobiography, *Finding Home: An Imperfect Path to Faith and Family.* Jim Daly has been the president and CEO of Focus on the Family since 2005.[2]

We want so badly to get it all right—our marriages, our parenting, our family dynamics. We want to meet all the requirements of a good Christian family. But God takes every hour of our home life, as well as every hour outside of it, and he uses the mistakes, the flaws, the pain as much, if not more, than he uses the good.

This is not license to sweep away our concerns about our family's well-being. "Shall we go on sinning so that grace may increase?" Paul asked rhetorically. "By no means!" (Romans 6:1–2). We will account for every part of our lives. But we have to let go of this idea that the only way God will save and sanctify our children is if we do our part exactly right and create the perfect Christian home: the right size family, the right method of education and discipline, the right roles for husbands and wives, the right amount of church. The family *is* vitally important, but it is one means among others that God uses to shape his people and direct his purposes.

> We have to let go of this idea that the only way God will save and sanctify our children is if we do our part exactly right and create the perfect Christian home.

A FAMILY REUNION

When we are disappointed with our families here and now, or simply feel out of place, we need not dwell in feelings of failure.

This is not the end. Jesus promises us a home in heaven and a family reunion unlike anything we've ever known. He has gone "to prepare a place" for us in his "Father's house" (John 14:2). The book of Revelation gives us a vision of that home. Down from a restored heaven it comes, a city prepared as beautifully as a bride on her wedding day. As the city descends, God announces a new order, a new home, a new family:

> Now the dwelling of God is with men, and he will live
> with them. They will be his people, and God himself
> will be with them and be their God.... He who over-
> comes will inherit all this, and I will be his God and
> he will be my son. (Revelation 21:3, 7)

Can you imagine that day, when multitudes gather from every culture, ethnicity, era, and tribe? People called from innumerable families brought together in a single family. Parents, spouses, orphans, singles, widows, children—every role and relationship renewed in the burning light of God's glory. We are sisters and brothers inhabiting God's own house always.

I pray that we can parent with this vision before us. But we're not there yet. Our earthly families will be formed in a variety of ways, across cultures and generations, with this one constant: we will always be imperfect. We will always experience change, challenges, and incompleteness, all of which leads us to long for what is coming. This is the condition of every human family. This is the condition of this present world, which stands leaning like a "windblown porch" on the perfect, stately house of heaven.[3]

As we stand on our windy porches, leaning together toward the front door, let us extend grace to ourselves and one another. Soon that door will open and we will enter the Father's perfect family, where we will forever belong.

For Reflection and Discussion

1. How is your family similar to other families in your community? In what ways is it different?

2. Describe a time when you felt that someone else was judging you because your family was imperfect or unusual in some way.

Read Genesis 45:1–28.

3. How did God use the weaknesses of Joseph's family for good?

4. Why do you think God used such a broken family to found the new nation of Israel?

5. Describe a time when you've seen God at work in or through a family despite the personal shortcomings of its members.

Read 1 Corinthians 12:17–26.

6. What do these verses suggest about honoring different types of families within God's community?

7. How would your attitude toward your family life change if you believed God was using your family despite its differences or limitations?

Read John 14:2–3.

8. Why do you think Jesus used the imagery of a house when describing heaven? How might the promise of the Father's house have comforted his disciples?

9. How does your hope of heaven influence your parenting today?

The Holy Enterprise
of Parenting

We had just arrived at fish camp—a remote island off the west side of Kodiak Island where Duncan and I have lived and commercial fished for more than three decades. Every summer, our family alone inhabits the island as we harvest salmon, pulling them from our nets in stormy seas in a grueling three- to four-month season.

It was early June. I was in the house, unpacking, when I heard a sound of distress. I stepped out of the house and began walking down the gravel path, looking for the source of the sound, when I saw Noah. He was lying on the ground, writhing in pain. I ran to his side. His face was deeply abraded, partly crushed and bleeding; his leg looked broken. He could hardly speak. I saw the ATV at the foot of the hill and knew what happened. He had been riding without a helmet and lost control while going down the steep hill. He had smashed into a tree—with his face and leg bearing the brunt of the impact.

The fog was so thick that day the Coast Guard could not send a helicopter to medevac him to the hospital, but one pilot heard the emergency call and put his own float plane in the water to get to us. An hour and half later, I knelt on the floor of a four-seater bush plane beside my thirteen-year-old son, who was now lying strapped to a plank to hold his head and neck still. I wanted to lie there in his place. Seven-month-old Micah sat in his infant seat on my other side. The fog was so impenetrable we could see nothing out our windows. At one point, just minutes into the flight, we banked a hard, nearly vertical turn, flattening me to the floor. *A mountain. We're going to hit a mountain,* I thought as I gripped both sons' arms.

We missed the mountain. We made it to the hospital. Noah healed from his injuries. But I will not forget that flight. In those dramatic moments, as I lay nearly spread-eagled over my boys, sure we would crash, I experienced an unexpected peace. I knew with a cell-deep certainty that their lives, and the lives of my children back at camp, were gifts from God. I knew that these children were created to serve God and fulfill his great and mysterious purposes.

> This is the greatest parenting truth I can know: my children belong to God.

As I look back on that day, I realize that this is the greatest parenting truth I can know: my children belong to God. This is also the most difficult truth to live out in my everyday parenting life as I navigate a different kind of wilderness at home. Like all families, our home life is a jumble of tempests, celebrations, chaos, and love. Last night, Abraham and Micah wrote "I love you, Mom" on dozens of sticky notes and pasted them all over the floor of my office and on my back as I sat at my computer writing this chapter. At breakfast this morning, after polite conversation with me, one son started teasing another to tears. Another son bid me a good day, then headed out to school where he is hanging out with a new set of kids I don't know. Later my daughter called from college to thank me for a package I sent and to share her struggle with a serious theological issue.

I can still feel it at times—almost a panic. A fog. *Will my children make the right choices? Will they become the kind of people I hope they will become? Am I loving them enough? Do I sacrifice enough? Am I making huge parenting mistakes? Am I making a series of small mistakes? How will I know if I'm failing? How will I know if we are going to crash?*

But more and more I am able to remember the truths I knew on the plane that day, the truths I've absorbed through studying the Scriptures, the truths that go against my culture and my own sins and insecurities to bring me to the feet of

Jesus. The yoke I've hoisted on my own back has been heavy, but God's yoke is light! He is my sin-bearer, my care-carrier, my alpha and omega who knows the beginning from the end and who accomplishes his glorious will through every child he gave me.

I have new peace and new strength—and a new companion for the journey. God is here with me in this beautiful everyday riot of my house and my heart. He is with me as my redeemer, my sovereign, and also as a parent himself, a Father who has revealed his own tender, hurting, hope-filled heart. I know now that parenting is not meant to paralyze me with guilt but to send me running freely to God. Parenting is not meant to cripple me with insufficiency but to lead me to God's sufficiency. Parenting is so much less about me and so much more about God! This is God's holy enterprise—and wondrously, joyously, I get to be a part of it.

Now I am able, even in the midst of the questions and delights of a parent, to return to the highest call upon my life: to love God with all that I have and all that I am. I hope to teach my children the same. Together we can marvel at this sovereign God, this fiercely devoted heavenly parent, this loving, holy Father who will one day call us to live with him in his perfect, unending home.

For Reflection and Discussion

1. Describe a time when you had a sense of peace about your child belonging to God.

2. What would it look like in your life this week to let parenting be more about God and less about you than it has been in the past?

3. How have your views of parenting changed through reading this book?

4. Which myth in this book is most difficult for you to let go of? Why?

5. What is most freeing to you about exchanging these parenting myths for the truth?

6. What specific change(s) will you make in your parenting as a result of this book?

Notes

Parenting Doesn't Have to Be This Hard

1. Focus on the Family Web site, "Why Are Parents So Quick to Criticize Themselves?" http://family.custhelp.com/cgi-bin/family.cfg/php/enduser/prnt_adp.php?p_faqid=698&p_ (accessed June 18, 2008).

2. Julie Ann Barnhill, *Motherhood: The Guilt That Keeps on Giving* (Eugene, OR: Harvest House, 2006), 5–6.

Myth 1: Having Children Makes You Happy and Fulfilled

1. Susan Douglas and Meredith Michaels, *The Mommy Myth: The Idealization of Motherhood and How It Has Undermined All Women* (New York: Free Press, 2004), 3–4.

2. Leslie Leyland Fields, *Surprise Child: Finding Hope in Unexpected Pregnancy* (Colorado Springs, CO: WaterBrook Press, 2006).

3. See "The Cost of Raising Children," MSN Money, http://moneycentral.msn.com/articles/family/kids/tlkidscost.asp; "Cost of Raising Children Calculator," ABC News, http://abcnews.go.com/Business/page?id=4019746.

Myth 2: Nurturing Your Children Is Natural and Instinctive

1. Intuitive Parenting, "What Is Intuitive Parenting?" www.intuitiveparenting.org (accessed August 26, 2006).

2. *Marvin's Room,* directed by Jerry Zaks (New York: Miramax Film, 1996).

3. Marilynn Marchione for the Associated Press, "Wounded GI Endures Blindness, Paralysis," *Washington Post,* June 24, 2007, http://www.washingtonpost.com/wp-dyn/content/article/2007/06/24/AR2007062401065.html (accessed May 6, 2008).

4. Susan Dentzer, "Revisiting a Wounded Warrior," *Online NewsHour,* December 26, 2005, http://www.pbs.org/newshour/bb/middle_east/july-dec05/soldier_12-26.html (accessed May 6, 2008).

5. Marchione, "Wounded GI Endures Blindness, Paralysis."

Myth 3: Parenting Is Your Highest Calling

1. June Fuentes, "True Worship Unto Him," entry on A Wise Woman Builds Her Home blog, posted December 3, 2006, http://proverbs14verse1.blogspot.com/2006/12/true-worship-unto-him.html (accessed May 18, 2008).

2. For example, Kerby Anderson of Probe Ministries writes in "The Decline of a Nation," that "Families are the foundation of a nation. When the family crumbles, the nation falls because nations are built upon family units. They are the true driving social force. A nation will not be strong unless the family is strong." As found at

http://www.leaderu.com/orgs/probe/docs/decline.html (accessed June 15, 2007).

3. Dorothy Patterson, "The High Calling of Wife and Mother in Biblical Perspective" in *Recovering Biblical Manhood and Womanhood,* ed. John Piper and Wayne Grudem (Wheaton, IL: Crossway, 2006), 367. Also online at http://www.leaderu.com/orgs/cbmw/rbmw/chapter22.html (accessed May 30, 2008).

4. Pierre Thomas, "Rise in Child Abuse Called National 'Epidemic,'" *ABC News,* April 25, 2005, http://abcnews.go.com/print?id=701293 (accessed May 30, 2008).

Myth 4: Good Parenting Leads to Happy Children

1. Tara Parker-Pope, "A One-Eyed Invader in the Bedroom," *New York Times,* March 4, 2008, http://www.nytimes.com/2008/03/04/health/04well.html (accessed May 13, 2008).

2. Aleksandra Todorova, "Overspending on Kids Risks Parents' Financial Future," *SmartMoney,* June 6, 2007, as quoted at "Parents Gone Wild (for Their Kids)," MSN Money, July 3, 2007, http://articles.moneycentral.msn.com/CollegeAndFamily/RaiseKids/ParentsGoneWildForTheirKids.aspx (accessed May 15, 2008).

3. Bob Sullivan, "Blame the Kids for All That Red Ink," MSNBC, December 13, 2005, http://redtape.msnbc.com/2005/12/why_are_america.html (accessed May 13, 2008).

4. J. Hampton Keathley III, "The Principle of Nurture (Training Your Child)," Bible.org, http://www.bible.org/page.php?page_id=1379 (accessed May 13, 2008).

5. Michael and Debi Pearl, *To Train Up a Child* (Pleasantville, TN: No Greater Joy Ministries, 1994), 83.

6. David Wells, "The Bleeding of the Evangelical Church," *Founders Journal* 63 (winter 2006): 25–33. This article is available online at Founders Ministries, http://www.founders.org/FJ63/article3.html (accessed September 5, 2006).

7. Wells, "The Bleeding of the Evangelical Church."

Myth 5: If You Find Parenting Difficult, You Must Not Be Following the Right Plan

1. Michael and Debi Pearl, *To Train Up a Child* (Pleasantville, TN: No Greater Joy Ministries, 1994), 8, 46–47.

2. Gary Ezzo and Robert Bucknam, *On Becoming Baby Wise: The Classic Sleep Reference Guide Used by Over 1,000,000 Parents Worldwide* (Sisters, OR: Parent-Wise Solutions, 2001).

3. Pearl and Pearl, *To Train Up a Child*, 2.

4. Reb Bradley, "Solving the Crisis in Homeschooling," updated and revised, Family Ministries, September 22, 2006, http://www.family ministries.com/HS_Crisis.htm (accessed May 16, 2008).

5. L. Elizabeth Krueger, "Teaching Obedience—Tomato Staking," Raising Godly Tomatoes, http://www.raisinggodlytomatoes .com/ch07.asp (accessed May 31, 2008).

6. L. Elizabeth Krueger, "Teaching Obedience—The Basics and Before," Raising Godly Tomatoes, http://www.raisinggodly tomatoes.com/ch03.asp (accessed May 16, 2008).

7. *On Becoming Baby Wise: The Classic Sleep Reference Guide Used by*

Over 1,000,000 Parents Worldwide by Gary Ezzo and Robert Bucknam has garnered 991 reviews on amazon.com as of May 31, 2008.
Healthy Sleep Habits, Happy Child by Marc Weissbluth has received
1,099 reviews on amazon.com as of May 31, 2008.

8. Dr. Tim Kimmel, *Why Christian Kids Rebel: Trading Heartache for
Hope* (Nashville: W Publishing Group, 2004), 26.

9. Bradley, "Solving the Crisis in Homeschooling."

10. Bradley, "Solving the Crisis in Homeschooling."

Myth 6: You Represent Jesus to Your Children

1. John Piper, entry on Desiring God blog, posted April 26, 2008,
http://www.desiringgod.org/Blog/1202_Children_Understand_the_
Universe_Before_They_Know_There_Is_One/ (accessed June 23,
2008).

2. Devin Hudson, entry on Grace Is the Point blog, sermon posted
September 10, 2006, http://graceisthepoint.blogspot.com/
2006_09_01_archive.html (accessed May 15, 2008).

3. Karl Barth, *Church Dogmatics,* vol. 3, part 4, *The Doctrine of Creation,* trans. A.T. Mackay, T.H.L. Parker, H. Knight, H.A. Kennedy,
J. Marks (London: T & T Clark International, 2004), 278.

4. Rochelle Melville, "Family Revolution," *Signs of the Times,* June
2007, http://www.signsofthetimes.org.au/archives/2007/june/
article2.shtm (accessed May 30, 2008).

5. Richard L. Strauss, "The Majesty of Motherhood," Bible.org,
http://www.bible.org/page.php?page_id=2669 (accessed May 31,
2008).

6. Michael and Debi Pearl, *To Train Up a Child* (Pleasantville, TN: No Greater Joy Ministries, 1994), 77, 83.

7. Pearl and Pearl, *To Train Up a Child,* 43–44.

8. Pam Griner, "Mixed Up," MotherWise.org, http://www.motherwise .org/templates/System/details.asp?id=37830&PID=455335 (accessed May 27, 2008).

Myth 8: Successful Parents Produce Godly Children

1. Reb Bradley, "Two Obstacles to Successful Parenting" excerpted from *Child Training Tips: What I Wish I Knew When My Children Were Young* (Foundation for Biblical Research, 2002). Accessed online at http://www.familyministries.com/obstacles.html (May 30, 2008).

2. David E. Pratte, "Raising Godly Children," The Gospel Way, 2004, http://www.gospelway.com/family/children-plan.php (accessed May 30, 2008).

3. George Barna, *Revolutionary Parenting: What the Research Shows Really Works* (Carol Stream, IL: BarnaBooks/Tyndale, 2007), back cover.

4. Barna, *Revolutionary Parenting,* 154.

5. Barna, *Revolutionary Parenting,* 22–23.

6. Barna, *Revolutionary Parenting,* 152.

7. John Rosemond, "Some Hard Facts About Child Rearing" in his syndicated column "Family Times," *The Washington Times,* June 17, 2007, http://www.washingtontimes.com/news/2007/jun/17/some-hard-facts-about-child-rearing/ (accessed May 30, 2008).

8. Harriet Lerner, *The Mother Dance: How Children Change Your Life* (New York: HarperPerennial, 1998), 7.

9. Barna, *Revolutionary Parenting,* xxi.

Myth 9: God Approves of Only One Family Design

1. Melissa Keen, "Called to the Home—Called to Rule," Vision Forum Ministries, June 16, 2004, http://www.visionforum ministries.org/issues/family/called_to_the_home_called_to_ r.aspx (accessed May 30, 2008).

2. Lori Smith, "Finding Home: Jim Daly on His Imperfect Path to Faith and Family," Crosswalk.com, http://www.crosswalk.com/ root/root/books/11556671/page0/ (accessed May 30, 2008).

3. George MacDonald, *The Musician's Quest,* ed. Michael R. Phillips (Minneapolis: Bethany House, 1984), 197. (Originally published in 1868 as *Robert Falconer* by Hurst and Blackett, London.)

About the Author

LESLIE LEYLAND FIELDS is the mother of six children—a daughter and five sons who range in age from five to twenty. She is the author-mother of six books as well: *Surprise Child: Finding Hope in Unexpected Pregnancy, Surviving the Island of Grace, Out on the Deep Blue, The Entangling Net,* and *The Water Under Fish.* Her essays have appeared in *The Atlantic, Orion, Image, Best Essays NW, On Nature: Great Writers on the Great Outdoors, Mama PhD, It's a Girl: Women Writers on Raising Daughters,* and numerous other publications. Fields teaches part-time in Seattle Pacific University's Master of Fine Arts program and during the summer works in commercial fishing with her family off their remote island in Alaska.

When not teaching or fishing, Fields travels widely and speaks at conferences, retreats, and universities on faith, learning, literature, and family. Her first serious adventure began thirty-one years ago when she married Duncan, a lawyer and fisherman. Since then, their adventures together have included roughing it in the Alaskan wilderness, world travel, commercial fishing, and the grandest adventure of all—parenting.

The Fields family lives on Kodiak Island, Alaska, on a cliff over the ocean with a backyard of bald eagles, whales, and stormy seas.

To learn more about Leslie Leyland Fields,
visit her Web site at www.leslie-leyland-fields.com.
You can also reach her by e-mail at
northernpen@alaska.com.

"EACH YEAR, more than three million women discover
themselves pregnant—at a hard time, the wrong time,
at a difficult place in their lives. I am one of those women...."

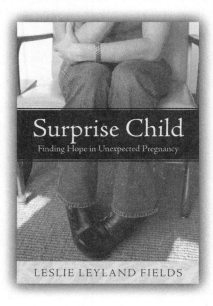

Surprise Child

Finding Hope in Unexpected Pregnancy

LESLIE LEYLAND FIELDS

If you know the isolation, discouragement, and confusion of an
unexpected pregnancy, *Surprise Child* will offer you practical help,
companionship, and real-life hope from women who have been
where you are.

Available in bookstores and from online retailers.

WATERBROOK PRESS
www.waterbrookpress.com